Anglican
Spirituality

William J. Wolf, editor

MOREHOUSE-BARLOW CO., INC. WILTON, CONNECTICUT

Morehouse-Barlow Co., Inc.
78 Danbury Road
Wilton, Connecticut 06897

ISBN 0-8192-1297-0

Library of Congress Catalog Card Number 81-84717

Printed in the United States of America

Table of Contents

Introduction

William J. Wolf

As a word "spirituality" suffers from indeterminancy at its edges, but it is used increasingly today to describe practice that makes religion come to life. Spirituality is "piety" or "devotion" that infuses the whole of life with prayer, worship and discipline. Its animating force is grace or the spirit of God "breathing" (in the origin of the word) upon the person. Jesus is reported in the Gospel of John as saying to the woman at the well: "God is spirit, and those who worship him must worship in spirit and truth" (John 4:24).

A word that might have been avoided by many ten years ago is increasingly on people's lips today. Sometimes there will be little direct reference to religion as such. Place is more and more being found in our culture for what it describes in the life styles of our contemporaries. One aspect of our religious situation today has been labeled "fast food spirituality." People want authentic religious experience and instant gratification for the impulse. This hunger has produced a strange smorgasbord. Spiritual practices are often cut off from their roots and from the disciplines and suffering needed to bring them to mature expression. A spirituality based on the principle of "to each his own" will inevitably be individualistic and as such false to the Biblical understanding of the human being as a part of a historical community of persons.

As members of the Episcopal Divinity School faculty, we want to address ourselves to this situation so common among our students today. We feel the same problems in ourselves. By trying to help others on a pilgrimage of authentic spirituality we may also be helping ourselves. We know the perils are many. We are not unaware of the gospel warning of the blind leading the blind and of the Pauline admonition against preaching to others and being castaways ourselves.

We are united in our conviction that the *Book of Common Prayer* presents a disciplined spirituality responsive to the Biblical revelation that over the centuries has shaped Anglican experience and practice. If in this journey the Bible can be considered the compass, ever calling the pilgrim back from false directions and pathways, then the *Book of Common Prayer* can be seen as a map, useless unless oriented to the true pole, but, if so pointed, a nearly indispensable roadguide. Intended for "common" or corporate worship, it is a means for bringing the individual into a holistic experience of worship. Such experience deepens individual use of the book and the repetition of personal experience builds up the individual for more effective participation in the corporate worship of God. A process of mutual fortification and reciprocal influence becomes operative and fruitful. The thought that we often become the kind of person we pray to become can be both comforting and devastating: comforting when we see it as God's way of educating the human race in Christian humanity, devastating if our piety is so self-centered and exploitative that it simply magnifies rather than heals these limitations in our character.

Frederick Maurice reflected this concern in classic comments on the Lord's Prayer addressed to those who shunned public worship thinking themselves to be obeying Christ's admonition to go into one's closet to pray. The passage has been adapted to the ecumenical version of the Lord's Prayer in the new prayer book and expresses a fundamental Anglican perspective in spirituality.

"When you are most alone you must still, if you would pray, be in the midst of a family; you must call upon a Father; you must not dare to say *my*, but *our*. Do you desire to be very holy? Yet this must not be your petition; you must say, 'Hallowed be *your* name.' Do you wish for some assurance of a heaven for yourself? Yet this must be your language: '*Your* kingdom come.' Do you wish to get some favorite project accomplished? It must be sought in this manner: '*Your* will be done on earth as in heaven.' Do you want a supply of your necessities, bodily or spiritual? Then you must desire the same for all your sisters and brothers, as well as for yourself: 'Give us today *our* daily bread.' Do you want forgiveness for your individual sins? The prayer is still, 'Forgive *us our* sins,' and the gift is only received when it is circulated, 'as we forgive those who sin against us.' Do you feel that your fellow creatures are your tempters? Yet you must acknowledge their temptations and yours to be the same; you must ask that they may not be led into the very temptations which they cause, else you will be their tempter as well as your own. And this because the evil from which you must pray to be delivered is a common evil, an evil which is the same in root and principle, though it may take innumerable forms; that very evil of selfishness, of individuality, which we are disposed to make our very prayers a means of seeking, and which will encompass us and possess us, if we do not learn to join the ascription: 'For the kingdom, the power, and the glory are yours' " *(The Kingdom of Christ,* Part II, Chap. IV, Section 3).

For Anglicans the *Book of Common Prayer* has itself been *the* devotional book. It is intended not just for clerics, but for every member. Anyone studying Anglican spirituality soon discovers this fact, but the actual impact of the *Book of Common Prayer* on Anglican spirituality often remains vague, unfocused and poorly articulated. The cultural impact of the *Book of Common Prayer* too is far more powerful than is known or acknowledged. Consider, for example, Handel's *Messiah,* by many thought to be the greatest piece of choral music in the English-speaking world. How many are aware that the scriptural passages follow the outline of the Church year including specific passages read as lessons at given points in that cycle, or even more dramatically, that Part III of the Oratorio about victory over death follows in its choice of Biblical materials the sequence of these passages in the Prayer Book Order for the Burial of the Dead?

It is the underlying influence of the *Book of Common Prayer* on spirituality that among other themes we will try to make more concrete in this book. If that impact is as pervasive and dynamic upon Anglican spirituality as we believe it has been and still is, then obviously a new dimension presents itself. While the Bible is a completed book, the *Book of Common Prayer* from time to time must be revised to keep it relevant to God's people on their pilgrimage through human history and the world of nature. Anglicans have sometimes confused the status of the prayer book and the Bible and have stoutly fought against revision of the former. While this resistance sometimes degenerated into an idolatrous worship of the book ("our incomparable liturgy") instead of the God to whom the book is meant to point, the resistance is itself testimony to the powerful shaping forces of the prayer book upon Anglican spirituality corporate and personal.

Other Christians were sometimes surprised that the "death of God" movement of a decade or so ago made so little headway among Anglicans. What did bring Episcopalians out of their corners, however, was the "death of the prayer book" during the long process of revision leading to the new official *Book of Common Prayer* of 1979. This revision has been much more fundamental and radical than any of the previous books (1928, 1892, 1789, 1662, 1559) until we reach the founding revisions of 1549 and 1552. A new prayer book, especially one with many options, implies new spiritualities.

The extensive nature of the changes in the 1979 book force Anglicans to achieve a new understanding of the problems of continuity and change. The time is ripe for a contemporary treatment of *Anglican Spirituality*. We undertake it as members of a faculty who worship according to the new book, discussing its impact on us in the midst of our concerns about world hunger, sexism, justice, peace and the environment.

Our predecessors in this place in 1924 wrote *Creeds and Loyalty*, a faculty manifesto called forth by controversies of that period. We hope that this faculty effort in 1982 will be helpful as we enter the so-called "age of diminishment." In the confusion today about "spirituality" we want to point to a spirituality responsive to the love of God and love of neighbor.

In the first chapter Harvey Guthrie describes Anglican spirituality and examines such issues as its liturgical setting, spiritual direction, and the *Book of Common Prayer* as a *genre* comparable to the Rule of St. Benedict or to Bonhoeffer's *Life Together*. David Siegenthaler discusses some of "The Literature of Anglican Spirituality" in chapter two with special attention to spiritual tracts, devotional manuals, poetry, diaries and the biographies of saints. In chapter three John Booty studies contrition in Hooker, Donne and Herbert showing us that we have lost their understanding of contrition as the work of God's love in our current minimizing of the penitential note in public worship in favor of a happier atmosphere. In the fourth chapter, I bring together biography, theology, ethics, poetry, mysticism and saintliness to describe "The Spirituality of Thomas Traherne." In chapter five, John Booty presents an historical and theological survey of "Anglican Spirituality from Wilberforce to Temple" with special emphasis on participation, the law of sacrifice, the

Incarnation and the dichotomy between this world and the next world. Special attention is given to Newman, Maurice, Temple and Underhill. Daniel Stevick, in chapter six entitled "The Spirituality of the Book of Common Prayer," analyzes six of its major characteristics, underlines again the dominating importance of the liturgical orientation of Anglicanism, and suggests that while there is one authorized *Book of Common Prayer* there may and should be many spiritualities. Alastair Cassels-Brown in chapter seven describes "Music As an Expression of Anglican Spirituality" and concludes that it is an unofficial sacrament of the church. In chapter eight, "An Incarnational Spirituality," John Skinner describes a spirituality responsive to the Incarnation using the process philosophy of Whitehead as a conceptual foundation, thus continuing work in this area already started by William Temple, Lionel Thornton, Norman Pittenger and others. In an Afterword, I locate the consensus among the authors chiefly in the liturgical orientation of Anglican spirituality, but with special attention to continuing themes and their various resolutions and relate the findings to Anglicanism as a whole.

I

Anglican Spirituality: An Ethos and Some Issues

Harvey H. Guthrie

What "Anglican" means is very hard to define. As I think about trying, places and people significantly different from one another—everyone of which is in fact Anglican—come to mind. I think of St. Andrew's Abbey in Denver, Colorado, where going to the liturgy on Sunday not too long ago was to find oneself in a very up to date equivalent of a Benedictine establishment centuries old. Yet, I think also of the cathedral in Sydney, Australia, where there is no altar but a plain, wooden table, and where doctrine and ethos are about as Protestant as can be conceived. I think of the bishop of the recently become independent diocese of Puerto Rico who is very Latin in temperament and style and flair, of the bishop of Maseno South in Kenya who is very African in tribal origin, speech and loyalty, of the archbishop of New Zealand in whom British crispness and Oxford acerbity and Maori astuteness all dwell together, of the primate of the United States whose accent is very southern and who is seen as pretty conservative, of the primate of Canada whose accent is very north-of-the-border and who is seen as fairly liberal. I think of a lawyer in the southwestern part of the United States who goes to a high church mass everyday and who has defended civil rights advocates and anti-Vietnam war protesters, of a banker who goes to Morning Prayer only and who would consider protest of any kind as well as prodding into his spiritual life as indecent, of a New England nurse who is a born-again Christian with a well-thumbed Good News Bible in her hands, of a priest who teaches comparative literature and whose spirituality is very Zen, of a nursery school teacher who is a faith healer.

I could go on. Anyone at all familiar with the Anglican churches who thinks about it could come up with a list of contrasts seeming to indicate the impossibility of arriving at any comprehensible definition of "Anglican." I do, however, believe that there is

1

indeed something finally—if vaguely—indentifiable as "Anglican" if we will allow that which is being identified to provide the terms of the identification, if we will not presume to impose upon it terms originating in other realities. Furthermore, I believe that other Anglicans, in spite of the vast differences among us, would agree with me that there is something identifiable as "Anglican." We might define it differently, but we would have in common our assumption that there is an "it" to define: an "it" which means a great deal to us both individually and corporately, an "it" which keeps us in the fellowship even when we find ourselves disagreeing with almost every decision taken by the official bodies of our Church, an "it" which has attracted a high percentage of us into one of the Anglican churches out of many different ecclesiastical and secular backgrounds. Moreover, for reasons I shall outline later on, I believe it to be extremely important for those of us who are Anglicans to seek to arrive at a definition of "Anglican" at this point in our history at which so many new realities have to be taken into account.

An Ecclesiastical Typology

Someone, located so far back there in my life that I have forgotten who it was, taught me one of those simplistic lessons easy to remember but probably not adequate to the complicated nature of any reality. The lesson was that there have been, down through Christian history, three basic manifestations of the Church. Upon reflection, I believe that lesson does bear some relation to reality. The lesson had it that those three manifestations of the Church are distinguished from one another by the way in which each of them defines what constitutes membership in the Church.

The first type of church is *confessional*. It holds that what fundamentally makes one a part of the Church is one's confession of the faith which is held by the Church. In the understanding of this type of church, the Church is that body of people which confesses a common faith. The second type of church is *experiential*. It holds that what fundamentally makes one a part of the Church is one's having participated in that experience of conversion through which one's fellow Christians came into the body of those who have been saved by Christ. In the understanding of this type of church, the Church is that body of people who have individually undergone a common religious experience. The third type of church is *pragmatic*. It holds that what fundamentally makes one a part of the Church is one's doing with the Church what the Church does liturgically, sacramentally and empirically. In the understanding of this type of church, the Church is that body of people who have undergone baptism, who participate in the celebration of the Eucharist, who observe the Church's feasts, fasts and ordinances. In the understanding of this type of church individuals may hold various confessional positions, may have undergone differing religious experiences or no particular religious experience at all. The basic thing they have in common is neither a doctrinal position nor a religious experience. It is simply participating in what the Church does as Church.

As I see it, the Anglican churches are fundamentally churches of the third type. And, as I see it, therein lie both the strength and the weakness of Anglicanism. The questions with which Anglicans are characteristically concerned are pragmatic questions. They have to do with whether or not the sacraments are presided over by validly and regularly ordained ministers, with what vestments may properly and legally be worn on occasions of public worship, with whether or not the persons proposing to vote in a parish meeting have been baptized and have received communion at least three times during the past year and have supported the parish financially.

That approach to what constitutes membership in the Church certainly has its weak and trivial side. It produces arid and Erastian situations which drive disciples of the Wesleys to found the Methodist Church and which caused John Henry Newman to turn to the Church of Rome. That approach can result in a church which is theologically flabby, which seems constitutionally incapable of taking a stand on anything significant, which is inarticulate with regard to the demands of Christian faith in some given set of historical circumstances. It can result in a church which neither remembers nor knows any Christian experience which sets it apart from the world in which it exists. It can produce a church which is just the House of Lords or Wall Street or a secular university or some country club at prayer.

That approach also has, however, its steady and comprehensive and inclusive and catholic side. It is not narrowly sectarian. It is capable of transcending the kind of merely intellectual and ideological conceptions of Christianity which keep dividing the

Church into more and more numerous groups of believers holding more and more finely defined theological positions. It can thwart that spiritual arrogance which insists that true Christianity must involve only the particular kind of religious experience that I and those like me have undergone. It can allow for difference of opinion—even doctrinal opinion—within one, united Church. It can conceive of quite different parties being parts of one Christian fellowship. It can provide a place where folk busy with the world's real business and lacking time for theological fine points or rarified spiritual experience can pray in a matter-of-fact, eyes-open, no-nonsense kind of way.

It is that kind of approach which lies at the heart of distinctively Anglican spirituality. Distinctively Anglican spirituality is grounded in the ongoing, corporate, liturgical life of the Church participated in by lay people as well as clergy, by those with occupations in the world as well as those committed to the monastic life. Anglican spirituality arises out of the common prayer of a body of Christians who are united in their participation—through physical presence and liturgical dialogue and sacramental action—in the cult in which the Church identifies itself as Church. It involves a corporate life whose times and seasons and offices and ordinances and readings and sermons are the means of corporate participation, in and through Christ, with God present to and for human beings in history in this world. Private devotion and prayer and meditation on the part of individuals are supports for and means of putting oneself into and extensions of the ongoing, corporate, liturgical life of the Church.

Anglican spirituality is corporate and liturgical and sacramental. That is why, even though the Bible is so central to Anglican spirituality and is read extensively and regularly and serially in the office and the eucharistic liturgy, the Bible per se is not the basis of Anglican spirituality. Indeed, the Bible itself is never, purely and exclusively, the basis of any spirituality, even spiritualities which would think of themselves as biblical. Whether those reading it are conscious of the fact or not, the Bible is always read in some context. The Bible may be read in the context of some doctrinal position centering on the exclusive authority of the Bible. It may be read in the context of some conviction about the way in which the Bible speaks directly to the heart of the individual believer. It may be read in the context of various doctrinal or devotional presuppositions, but it is always read in some context. In

Anglicanism that context is the corporate, liturgical, sacramental life of the Church. The Bible is indeed central in Anglican spirituality, is used much more extensively in Anglican liturgy than it is in the worship of many churches more ideologically biblical in their orientation. The Bible itself, however, is not the *basis* of the Anglican spirituality.

Neither is some system of individual devotion or meditation the basis of Anglican spirituality. We are so much the products of the culture in which we live that we are, on the whole, unconscious of the extent to which modern, western anthropology is the framework within which the life of prayer and devotion, the spiritual life, is lived and understood. Modern, western anthropology is fundamentally individualistic and rationalistic. That which makes me what I really am is that which sets me apart from, "individuates" me from, other human beings. Furthermore, that which is most real about things and beings, from atoms to the Almighty, is what I think and feel about them, what they "mean." Those views of what I am and what I deal with have, for the most part quite unconsciously, dominated western spirituality from St. Ignatius and the classic German pietists to contemporary emphases on personal growth. For both Roman Catholic and Protestant spirituality in post-reformation, western Christianity, systems of individual devotion in which "mental prayer" is central have been dominant. The Church's liturgy, its offices and sacraments, have in reality been more resources for individual devotion than the central thing, have become overshadowed by the acts of individual preparation, individual participation and individual thanksgiving emphasized in instruction and manuals and practice.

Anglican spirituality, however, is basically corporate, liturgical and sacramental. That is why its basis is neither the Bible per se nor some system or manual of individual devotion and meditation. That is why the basis of Anglican spirituality is the *Book of Common Prayer*, that book belonging to both clergy and laity which is the means by which the corporate, liturgical and sacramental life of the Church is entered into and participated in by both clergy and laity. The *Book of Common Prayer*, in whatever edition of whatever branch of the Anglican Communion we may choose to examine it, is certainly an exceedingly eclectic collection of materials from many sources and many ages. That is true of both the older Prayer Books and the newer ones which provide various alternatives. Commentaries on the *Book of*

Common Prayer go to great lengths to trace the things that make
it up back to a thousand different origins, beginning with the Bible
itself. That serves to show how rich is the heritage underlying the
Prayer Book, as well as to show how the book is the result of a
complicated, living history in which many theological and ecclesiastical compromises have taken place.

The Nature of Prayer Book Spirituality

The more basic and important question, however, has to do
with what the Prayer Book is in its entirety and not just with where
its various parts may have originated. It has to do with the
ascetical *genre* of the *Book of Common Prayer*. Though it serves
a similar purpose as the *Missale Romanum*, the Prayer Book is
more than a missal. Though it serves the same purpose as the
Roman breviary, it is more than a breviary. We could go on in the
same kind of way about all the various parts of the Prayer Book,
the pastoral offices and the ordinal and the psalter and the
catechism. What the Prayer Book is consists of more than its
various parts and the functions they serve as liturgical manuals. It
is more than just a liturgical script for the doing of the Church's
offices, ordinances and sacramental actions.

The ascetical *genre* of the *Book of Common Prayer*, as Martin
Thornton so aptly observes in his *English Spirituality*, is the same
genre that finds expression in the Rule of St. Benedict, in
Bonhoeffer's *Life Together* which was written as the guide to the
corporate life of that underground seminary at Finkenwalde in the
time of the Third Reich, in the rule of various Christian
communities and monastic establishments. The ascetical *genre* of
the *Book of Common Prayer* is that of the *Regulum* which makes
it possible for the basis of the spiritual life of a community of
Christian people to be the corporate, liturgical, sacramental and
domestic life of that community itself. Whether they are explicitly
conscious of it or not, that is the fundamental *genre* of the Prayer
Book for Anglicans of either the low church or the high church
variety, of either the most catholic or the most evangelical
persuasion. That is the significance of the *Book of Common
Prayer* in a pragmatic Church which *de facto* defines both
"Church" and "Christian" in terms of a series of times observed, a
set of liturgical actions performed, a sacramental and corporate
life together. Anglican spirituality is Prayer Book spirituality in that

sense and it is the question of what Prayer Book spirituality is and implies in contemporary culture which must be addressed if Anglicans are to be responsible stewards of the heritage that is theirs. It is to that question that the remainder of this essay will address itself by pointing to a series of issues affecting the spiritual lives of Anglicans today.

Prayer Book Revision and Alternate Rites

One important issue has to do with the Prayer Book itself and the revision it has been undergoing in recent times in almost every branch of the Anglican Communion. Because Anglican spirituality is Prayer Book spirituality, it is a traumatic experience for Anglicans to have to put a much used and familiar book on the shelf and to begin to use a new one. What does it mean to speak of Prayer Book spirituality, if the Prayer Book is subject to radical change? Furthermore, if the Prayer Book is the *Regulum* enabling a community of Christian people to locate its spirituality in its own ongoing life, what are the implications of having a Prayer Book with various alternatives for celebrating the sacraments and observing the Church's ordinances? Given the nature of Anglicanism those are serious questions and advocates of change and modernization should not dismiss them lightly. They are connected with the profound way in which books and writing are so fundamental to the way in which western culture deals with reality and to the way in which the western churches dealt with the issues underlying the Reformation. They are also connected with the disintegration of what Marshall McLuhan, in his *The Medium is the Message*, called western culture's linear apprehension of reality.

It is tremendously significant that the Reformation and the invention of moveable type by Gutenberg were contemporaneous events. There are many ways in which the Reformation marked the end of an old era rather than the beginning of a new era. As the human community found accustomed social, political, economic and cultural configurations giving way to new ones, as new national identities emerged, the Reformation era was a time in which, in different ways and in different places, Christian people strove to preserve their heritage so that it would not be lost in the new cultural situation. It was a time for seeking what was essentially Christian as the historical structures which had

contained Christianity began to disappear, and it was a time for
seeking guarantees that the essentials would be maintained. As
different as were the classical Protestant, Roman Catholic and
Anglican responses to that time, they had one very significant
thing profoundly in common: each of them preserved the heritage
in a book; each of them sought to guarantee the maintenance of
the essentials by identifying the book which contained them.

For the classical Protestant churches that book was the Bible. It
is difficult for us to remember, given the place of the Bible as book
in western culture, that the Bible as we know it did not exist prior
to the Reformation and the invention of moveable type. People
knew the contents of the book now so available to everyone as
book by hearing the readings in the liturgy, by taking in the
narratives pictured in paintings, frescoes and stained glass,
through dramatic presentations and the reading of poetry.
Furthermore, it was only at the time of the Reformation, when the
Bible as book became so important, that explicit and official
ecclesiastical decisions were made as to just which writings
constituted the sacred book. Of course, going back into the early
centuries of the Church's life, a general consensus as to which
books were canonical had emerged. No final and explicit
decisions had, however, been promulgated, and there was
variation as to which writings were included and read. It was in
connection with the Reformation's concern to preserve the
Christian heritage in a book that the Protestant Churches officially
excluded from the Bible those books—the Apocrypha—found in
the Greek version of the Old Testament but not in the Hebrew,
while the Roman Catholic Church took the official stand that
those books were canonical. The Bible as the book which
authoritatively defined Christianity was the product of Protes-
tantism's response to the collapse of "Christendom" and
Gutenberg's invention of moveable type.

For Roman Catholicism the book was the *Missale Romanum*.
Before the era of the Reformation various rites were in existence
in the various areas of Europe, and the "scripts" for the parts
played in the liturgy by the various ministers existed separately. It
was out of the Reformation concern that the heritage be accu-
rately preserved and also the availability of moveable type, that
the liturgy in all its parts came to be standardized in one book. It
was that Reformation concern and post-Gutenberg printing
technology which led to the liturgy's becoming essentially the

reading by the priest of a text in a book while the faithful usually engaged in devotions read from their own books.

For Anglicanism the book which emerged from the Reformation was, of course, the *Book of Common Prayer*. What I have just said about the process underlying the creation of the Roman missal was also true of the process by which the Prayer Book came into existence, although all the Church's ordinances rather than just the eucharistic liturgy were included in the one Prayer Book and the book became the common property of both clergy and lay people in a way that the missal and the breviary did not in the Roman Church. Whereas participation in the liturgy had formerly involved seeing, hearing, touching and smelling, Anglicans' participation came characteristically to involve following in the book the text of what was being said.

All that is the background against which western Christian people of all kinds have undergone traumatic experiences in the recent past as historical research has shown how clearly the various books are the products of history and the complex life of the Church, not unconditioned sacred authorities. It is the background against which, to the extent that people do leave behind what McLuhan called linear consciousness, book-centered Christianity becomes an anachronism not really connected with people's modes of apprehending reality. It is the background which explains why revisions of Bibles, missals and Prayer Books result in controversy and resistance. It is the background against which revised Prayer Books containing a collection of doctrinal statements instead of one catechism or set of articles of religion and alternatives for doing the liturgy are confusing and disorienting to Church people.

Anglican spirituality being profoundly Prayer Book spirituality, that issue has to be addressed if we are to be responsible stewards of our heritage as Anglicans at this time in history. One way of addressing it may be to learn anew the significance of the fact that the fundamental *genre* of the Prayer Book is that of a *Regulum*, a rule such as the Rule of St. Benedict which is the basis on which a community of people do the things they do together. A Benedictine community does read and listen to its rule, but reading and hearing the words of the rule is not the essence of its life as a community. The essence of its life is what it *does* as a community liturgically, domestically and socially and at work. The rule does not exist to be read as an end in itself, but exists to lead the community corporately into what it *does* as a community. And that is what the *Book of Common Prayer* is for the Anglican churches. It does not exist to be read as an end in itself, in spite of the extent to which it came to be used in that way in western, "linear" culture. The Prayer Book is the basis on which the Church *does* what it does in things as different as a solemn mass at the abbey in Denver or a celebration at the north end of the communion table in the cathedral in Sydney. The essential thing is not the script and the exact words in the script. The script exists to support the essential thing and to make it possible. The essential thing is the drama itself, the liturgical action, what the Church *does*. What the various churches have in common as Church is the action they have in common, the shape of the liturgy by which they identify themselves as Church, not the reading of the same, exact script in so slavish a way that the script dominates what it came into being to support and serve.

Looking at it that way can help us to understand that Prayer Book revision calculated to allow the action itself to shine through is really quite in the spirit of what the Prayer Book, understood in terms of its *genre*, is all about. It can help us to understand that it is quite fitting that alternative scripts be provided to accompany the action. Indeed, I believe it would have been much more logical for the framers of the *American Prayer Book 1979* to have put *An Order for Celebrating the Holy Eucharist* (page 400) at the very beginning of the provisions for celebrating the Eucharist, and then followed it with Rite One and Rite Two. Then the form of the book would have been saying, "People of God, here is what the Church *does* when it gathers to identify itself liturgically as the Church, and then here are a couple of scripts in varying styles of English to use in doing it." That kind of approach, and this is the point I am concerned to make, can lead us deeper into that Anglican spirituality which is grounded in participating with the Church in what the Church does in the Eucharist, in the Office, in the various sacraments and ordinances. Prayer Book spirituality is not really about the book. It is about the corporate life of the people of God for whom the Prayer Book is God's graciously given *Regulum*.

Personal Devotion and Spiritual Direction

Another set of issues in need of being addressed if Anglican spirituality is to be understood involves individual, personal devotion and spiritual direction. There is widespread interest today in prayer and the life of the spirit and spiritual direction. Given that interest, it is important that spirituality and spiritual direction not be equated with one approach or one tradition, that we be mindful that the Anglican tradition has its own characteristics, is basically corporate, liturgical and sacramental rather than individualistic. In the Anglican tradition personal, individual devotion and spiritual direction are not central. They are not ends in and of themselves. Some system of personal meditation is not the center of the spiritual life. Participation in the corporate, liturgical and sacramental life of the Church is the center of the spiritual life.

Consequently, in the Anglican tradition personal devotions are essentially recollection, in the classical sense of that word in ascetical theology, of Baptism, the Eucharist, the Daily Office and the biblical story in which Baptism, the Eucharist and the Daily Office are grounded. Personal devotions are recollection of what the Church does corporately, of what the present point in the Church's calendar is, of the biblical story the Church is presently hearing in its liturgy. That comes through clearly in such classically Anglican manuals of personal devotion as Andrewes' *Preces Privatae*, Taylor's *Holy Living* and *Holy Dying*, Herbert's *The Temple*, and Donne's prayers and sermons and poems. Those, and we could cite many other examples from Anglican literature, are intimately related to the Prayer Book. They originate in and are not understandable apart from that corporate life of the Church regulated and enabled by the *Book of Common Prayer*. They are embodiments of a tradition in which the prayers and meditation of the individual Christian are basically the results of and musings upon that in which the individual Christian is participating in an ongoing way in the Church.

Personal devotions in the Anglican tradition, moreover, are not "churchy" recollection. The logic of a spirituality which presupposes the presence of God with the historical, human Church in what it does as an historical, human institution also insists on the presence of God in human history in general. If Anglican tradition's coupling of nation and Church, of society and God's kingdom can result in crass Erastianism, it can also result in a piety which discerns God's presence in all of life, in "the daily round and the common task." That is why recollection of the presence of

God in life in the world, the discipline of being mindful of that presence in specific situations and persons and needs, is more typical of Anglican spirituality than the kind of self-conscious and structured mental prayer present, for example, in Ignatian spirituality. Anglican spirituality, grounded in faith in the presence of God in the empirical Church and in the givenness of the real world, is not individualistic and subjective. It is ecclesiastical, social and holistic.

That is the reason that spiritual direction in the Anglican tradition is not something which takes place primarily in the relationship between a Christian and an individual director in a one to one relationship. Spiritual direction is, in Anglicanism, a broad based thing, and the term itself in the sense in which it is presently so widely used is not native to Anglicanism. In the Anglican tradition spiritual direction has to do with a large, clergy-laity, individual-corporate, private-public dialogue which takes place in many ways. Direction from God to the individual Christian comes in the liturgy, in sermons, in catechetical instruction which is an ongoing and not once-and-for-all process in the Anglican tradition, in life in the world. To the person looking for direction in living the Christian life, the classical Anglican response would be, "Enter into the life of the Church with eyes and ears and heart and mind open." The richness of Anglican spirituality will be missed if spiritual direction is defined as something taking place between two individuals, if spiritual direction turns out to be something influenced more than we may consciously realize by clinical and psychological models, if spiritual direction is an enterprise of *mine* for which Church and liturgy and Bible are really only "resources." The point is this, and it is central and fundamental: in Anglican tradition the Church itself in the totality of its life and liturgy is the primary spiritual director.

"Mutual Ministry"

Another issue present in that Prayer Book spirituality which is characteristic of Anglicanism has to do with the way in which the life of Christians in the Church—and in the world—is a *common* enterprise. The book which contains the *Regulum* is the *Book of Common Prayer* the property of all the people of God. In the Anglican tradition no special class of believers is in possession of knowledge or techniques or status to which common folk do not have access. Neither Eucharist nor Office is, in Anglican tradition, something which is peculiarly the property of the clergy and those committed to a monastic life. In the earliest version of the *Book of Common Prayer* the daily office was put into a form calculated to make the attendance of lay people working in the world possible. Strong Anglican tradition, and in certain provinces explicit canonical provision, insist that a priest cannot celebrate the sacrament of the Eucharist unless a minimal congregation be there to participate in the celebration. The principle established in the sixteenth century that all parts of the liturgy should be in the language of the people has continued as the expansion of the Anglican Communion has resulted in the majority of Anglicans in the world being no longer white: the Prayer Book has been translated into many different languages. The tradition that the Church is the whole people of God, laity as well as clergy, has been borne out in the provisions made for the governance of the Church in the various branches of the Anglican Communion. Laity not only have a voice and vote along with clergy, but in important matters have the power to veto decisions voted by bishops and other clergy and vice-versa.

What is true of the Prayer Book and of liturgy and of provisions for ecclesiastical governance is true also of things usually more strictly considered to constitute the life of devotion. Lay-clerical dialogue is typical of the various forms of teaching and spiritual guidance in the Anglican tradition, the catechetical form of question and response itself being significant. From Dame Julian of Norwich in the fourteenth century to such contemporary figures as Evelyn Underhill and C. S. Lewis there has been a constant succession of lay spiritual guides, and it is significant that *priestly* manuals of devotion and prayer do not appear in Anglicanism until the latter part of the nineteenth century when, their own heritage having been obscured in the eighteenth century, many involved in the Catholic revival looked to Rome for guidance and models. Classical Anglican manuals such as those of Lancelot Andrewes, Jeremy Taylor and William Law, however, are clearly written with the people of God as a whole—lay and clerical alike—in mind. That type of clerical devotion which sees the priest's spiritual life as something different from a lay person's, which ties the priest's spiritual life to the liturgical functions performed by a priest and produces such customs as daily masses which are really the priest's personal devotions, is not intrinsically Anglican, nor is the

more contemporary custom of "concelebration" which arises out
of similar presuppositions.

We have passed through an era in the history of the Church in
which both Catholics and Protestants have had it in common that
the word "church" was pretty largely equated with "clergy" and
the word "ministry" equated with the work of ordained and
professional ministers. Now, however, biblical studies and the
recovery of the earliest Church's understanding of its life and
liturgy indicate the way in which the people of God as a whole,
the Church itself as a corporate reality, is God's minister and
God's priest to the world. We are coming to see that it is within
such a context that the ministries and vocations of *all* members of
the Body of Christ have to be understood.

But that is not really something new. The earliest versions of the
Book of Common Prayer made that radically clear in the sixteenth
century against the background of the ecclesiastical and liturgical
situation out of which they emerged. The *American Prayer Book
1979* continues to make that clear in its emphasis in many
different ways on the participation of all orders of Christian people
in the Church's liturgy and life. That emphasis does not represent
something new. It is, rather, the recovery of something central in
the Anglican tradition of spirituality. It represents the continuation
of something fundamental to a tradition in which the common,
corporate life of the Church is itself the focus and the basis of the
spiritual life. Current discussions of the recovery of the ministry of
the diaconate, of the role of the laity in the Church, of what has
come to be called "mutual ministry," touch on something central
in Anglican Prayer Book spirituality.

Community in a Complex Society

The final issue I shall point to in this essay has to do with a pre-
supposition which underlies all that I have said about the ethos of
Anglicanism and the issues to which I have devoted discussion.
There is no question but that the kind of Anglican spirituality we
have been looking at requires for its very existence a regularly
gathered community of Christians. The *Regulum*, which is really
what the *Book of Common Prayer* is, has no meaning if it is not
lived out liturgically and otherwise in a concrete, corporate human
community. That is why Anglican spirituality has found its
classical incarnation in the kind of collegial establishment present

in English colleges and cathedrals, or in the parish community living geographically together in villages or neighborhoods. The world has, however, moved on for better or for worse. Changes in the historical, cultural and social realities which constitute the environment in which Christians live have located the lives of Christians elsewhere than in collegial chapels and village churches. Individual Christians who in other times and places might have found themselves existing within the concrete, corporate contexts of collegial chapels and village churches find themselves adrift, existing quite individually and not at all with any sense of corporateness in today's mobile and impersonal urban society. I have lived most of my adult life as part of a seminary community in which daily worship, at office and eucharist, has been in the Anglican tradition. Again and again, however, I have heard expressed the disillusionment of those who found that embodiment of Anglican tradition a wonderful thing, but also a thing left behind when they moved from seminary to life in today's society and today's Church.

The issue to which I am pointing has to be faced. At the beginning of this essay I said that the pragmatic nature of Anglicanism—in which spirituality is connected with the Church's pragmatic, historical and incarnate life—can have its trivial and weak side. One form of that triviality and weakness can be the identification of the Church so completely with one, particular, historical incarnation that it ends up being an antiquarian anachronism, something perceived as utterly irrelevant and without value when social and cultural conditions have changed. That will not, in my view, do. Neither, however, will it do for Anglicans too easily or too quickly to espouse approaches to spirituality which are essentially individualistic and rational, which are—to use my earlier ecclesiastical typology—either confessional or experiential. Because the depth of the crisis which we face is so deep, I see all those alternatives being chosen: a traditional approach which defines the Church in terms of one historical incarnation, an evangelicalism which abandons Anglicanism for a confession of faith which is really more the heritage of other children of the Reformation, a neo-pentecostalism which makes religious experience of one type or another the norm.

My plea is that we do not take the demise of one particular set of structures to be the demise of the Anglican tradition. I believe that the collapse of those given national and geographical struc-

tures within which Anglicanism originally defined itself and continued to exist from the Reformation into contemporary times
provide an opportunity for the discovery of Anglicanism at a
deeper level. The kind of human community for which the reality
and existence of the human community itself is primary, both
enriched by and taking precedence over the confessional understandings of what it means and the experiences which have
brought people into it, is what this pluralistic, contemporary world
sorely needs. It is in terms of that kind of human community that
Anglicanism, the Prayer Book spirituality and ethos of Anglicanism, have to be understood. The vocation of Anglicans today
is to translate such an understanding, in parishes and "at work"
and "house church" and all kinds of other embodiments of the
Church, into the reality which God has given them as their
contribution to the Church Universal.

II

The Literature
Of
Anglican Spirituality

David Siegenthaler

Where does one find the literature of Anglican spirituality? What are the documents, the records, the aids, the guides for a comprehension of the spirituality of Anglicanism? The literature of Anglican spirituality is where you find it, or, somewhat more specifically, the literature of Anglican spirituality is found wherever Anglicans are writing in response to the experience of God.

For the purpose of this overview of that literature, *spirituality* is taken to be synonymous with *devotion* or *piety*, whether corporate or individual. It is used to designate reflection upon and response to the experience of God's presence in human life. For the same purpose, *Anglican* is used to designate that grouping of Christians whose ethos and spiritual life are derivative of the Church of England: possibly now jurisdictionally independent of that church, and separate from it in geography and ethnicity, to be sure, but, even so, standing in that continuum which takes its source in the Church of England and extends now around the world.

In thinking about Anglican spirituality one must be cautioned at the outset against either exclusivist or comparative thinking. Anglican spirituality is not unique. It shares much—giving and receiving—with the spirituality of other Christian groups. Nor is it useful to attempt value comparisons with other Christian spirituality, as if the object of the study were to find ways in which Anglican spirituality is better than some other. No, Anglican spirituality must be looked at and acknowledged and affirmed for what it is, regardless of the nature and characteristics of other spirituality: a style of devotion with roots in one place, yet adapted to and shaped by many other places.

It is also useful to keep in mind in approaching Anglican spirituality that it is characteristic of it that personal, individual spirituality seems always to flow from the corporate experience of God in public worship and in community. The *Book of Common Prayer* is informative for Anglicans not only for definition of doctrine and polity but as well for the content and style of spirituality. That book is the matrix. The concerns and consequences of corporate worship are the concerns and consequences of personal worship. In its simplest terms this means that Anglican spirituality is personal but never private, never detached from an individual's engagement with the community and with the world. Anglican spirituality seems always—as do the services of the *Book of Common Prayer*—to compell the individual back into the world. The person's individual needs for refreshment and enlightenment are not neglected in Anglican spirituality; but the matter is not left at that. The individual is empowered to rejoin the ranks of the larger company, to go forth in concert with others, to "continue in that holy fellowship, and do all such good works as God has prepared for us to walk in." (The post-communion thanksgiving from the *Prayer Book 1928* remains one of the splendid statements of this principle.)

The Church of England, and by extension, Anglicanism, began taking shape as a distinct constituent of the church catholic during the course of the sixteenth and seventeenth centuries. Its roots and those of its spirituality, however, extend to previous centuries of the Christian era. The roots of its spirituality are traced and their development is described in Martin Thornton, *English Spirituality* (London: SPCK, 1963), a comprehensive treatment of Christian spirituality in its English manifestation. C. J. Stranks, *Anglican Devotion: studies in the spiritual life of the Church of England between the Reformation and the Oxford Movement* (Greenwich: Seabury, 1961) is particularly valuable as a chronicle of the years leading to the eighteenth and nineteenth centuries, the centuries of the emergence of both the evangelical movement and the catholic revival in the Church of England. A useful collection of selections from the writings on worship, prayer, the sacraments, and the like of the earlier shapers of Anglicanism is found in *Anglicanism: the thought and practice of the Church of England, illustrated from the religious literature of the seventeenth century*, edited by Paul Elmer More and Frank Leslie Cross (London: SPCK, 1935). The selections are arranged topically and are accompanied by biographical notes. Of the great company of English spiritual writers before the sixteenth century, two have been published recently in very useful paper back editions. Each, in a different way, affords a clear view into an aspect of significant pre-reformation English spirituality. The first is Dame Julian of Norwich, *The Revelations of Divine Love* (New York: Image Books, 1977), and the second is Walter Hilton, *The Scale of Perfection* (St. Meinrad, Indiana: Abbey Press, 1975).

To look more specifically at the literature of Anglican spirituality and keeping in mind the definitions of those words given above, a further definition would suggest that the literature of Anglican spirituality is anything useful for devotional purposes, reflective of and in response to the experience of God, by anyone consciously writing from an Anglican perspective. There scarcely is room or time to list all the literature encompassed by that. What can be done, however, is to suggest categories of literature and cite some examples.

Spiritual tracts, of course, come first to mind. These are essays, treatises, short or long, of the sort which appeared in the authorized primer of 1553,[1] under the title "A Preparative unto Prayer." In the main such tracts deal with how one readies oneself to respond to the experience of God rather than provide words or sentiments for that response. A classic example of this kind of literature is William Law (1686-1761) *A Serious Call to a Devout and Holy Life* (New York: Paulist Press, 1978). (This volume appears as part of a commendable new series published by the Paulist Press, *The Classics of Western Spirituality*, which includes Jewish, Muslim and Native American works as well as Christian.) Two other "classics" are the companion works by Jeremy Taylor (1613-1667) *The Rule and Exercises of Holy Living* (Cleveland: World, 1956) and *The Rule and Exercises of Holy Dying* (Cleveland: World, 1952).

Devotional manuals form a second category, usually containing prayers and texts to be appropriated for use rather than—as tracts customarily do—suggesting ways of getting ready to respond. To some extent, the *Book of Common Prayer* is a devotional manual for individual as well as for corporate use, providing as it does specific language for specific occasions. As such, it is an invaluable aid in those times when our own words fail us. Mention above of the Primer 1553 brings to mind the great number of books of prayers and of little "offices" intended for individual use. They are part of a grand heritage. The Primer 1553 was successor to the Primer 1545 which, in turn, was type of the devotional manual so prevalent in earlier centuries and which customarily is called a Book of Hours. John Donne (1571-1631) composed his *Devotions upon Emergent Occasions* (Ann Arbor: University of Michigan, 1959, bound with his *Death's Duel*) very much in the tradition of the devotional manual, and there has been no dearth of similar volumes down to and including the present time. From the outset, Anglican devotional writers were aware of their linkage with the past and made generous use of the spirituality of previous centuries, at times appropriating and at times adapting older texts. A notable example is John Cosin (1594-1672), scholar, bishop and Prayer Book revisor, whose *Collection of Private Devotions in the Practice of the Ancient Church* (Oxford: Clarendon Press, 1967) first appeared in 1627. Its title page declares that the contents are ". . . taken out of the Holy Scriptures, the Ancient Fathers, and the divine Service of our own Church."

The prayers and texts of the best of these devotional manuals convey the author's own experience, something of the author's own struggle to perceive and respond to the presence of God. They are a useful resource for strengthening and refining one's own responsiveness. Even so, a devotional manual may not "work" for everyone. The only test of the usefulness of a piece of spiritual literature is whether it helps or hinders its reader, and what helps one may well hinder another.

Poetry occupies a prominent place in the literature of Anglican spirituality. John Donne (1571-1631), cited above, and George Herbert (1593-1633), especially "The Temple," together with the other "Metaphysical Poets,"[2] expressed in poetic form a profound awareness of the purchase of God upon their lives and the animating and motivating consequences of the Divine grasp. W. H. Auden and T. S. Eliot in more recent times have been informed and shaped by their Anglicanism and expressed their faith and spirituality in poem and prose. *The Hymnal 1940* is a treasury of the poetry of Anglican spirituality, as are its supplements. Notable among Anglican authors of the past whose poetry is included are Thomas Ken (1637-1711), Charles Wesley (1707-1788), William Cowper (1731-1800) and John Keble (1792-1866).

Anglican worship, corporate and individual, nourishes and enriches the day-to-day living of worshippers, fitting them for and sending them back into the world. The spirituality engendered by Anglican worship is no less integral a part of daily living. An important category of the literature of Anglican spirituality, consequently, is the records of those lives: the diaries, autobiographies and biographies of women and men, rooted in their Anglicanism, who acted out their daily lives conscious of God's continuous presence. This is, to be sure, the stuff of *hagiography*, the lives of the saints. Anglicanism does not lack for such faithful people. A few examples come readily to mind. The diaries of John Evelyn (1620-1706) published in the Everyman's Library by E. P. Dutton, chronicle the fortunes of the Church of England and their effect upon its members during the troubled years of political and ecclesiastical restoration following the Puritan interregnum of Oliver Cromwell. Robert Francis Kilvert (1840-1879) was a country parson in nineteenth century Wales. Selections from the diaries of his latter years, published under the title *Kilvert's Diary 1870-1879* (New York: Macmillan, 1947), bespeak his devotion and his perceptive and sympathetic regard for the world and the people around him. During her long life, Hannah More (1745-1833) wrote spiritual tracts and engaged in a variety of social and humanitarian causes, notably popular education and abolition of slavery. To read an account of her life, such as the one by M. G. Jones (Cambridge University Press, 1952) is to catch sight of the richness of her spirituality and the strength of it as a motivating force in her daily living. Hannah More was a member of the Clapham Sect[3] which included the great English reforming and abolitionist statesman William Wilberforce (1759-1833). His tract, "An Appeal to the Religion, Justice and Humanity of the Inhabitants of the British Empire" (reprinted New York: Negro Universities Press, 1969), is put into the context of the faithfulness of his life by reference to his biography, as, for example, the recent one by John Pollock, *Wilberforce* (London: Constable, 1977). Another example of the Christian as politician is William Ewart Gladstone (1809-1898). Like Wilberforce, Gladstone has had many biographers, Peter Stansky, *Gladstone: a progress in politics* (Boston: Little, Brown, 1979) being a current example.

The present century does not lack for Anglicans whose lives have been informed and vivified by their spirituality. Vida Dutton Scudder (1861-1954), professor of English and proponent of the Social Gospel, has in her autobiography *On Journey* (New York: Dutton, 1937) evidenced how deeply her life was permeated by her spirituality. Frances Perkins (1882-1965), secretary of labor in President F. D. Roosevelt's Cabinet, is another example. Her

faithfulness as a communicant of the Church was part and parcel
of the rhythm of her life as reference to a current biography,
George Martin, *Madam Secretary: Frances Perkins* (Boston:
Houghton Mifflin, 1976) indicates. Trevor Huddleston's *Naught
for Your Comfort* (Garden City: Doubleday, 1956) is at once both
a telling of his work in South Africa and a reflection of the
centrality in his life of his Anglican spirituality.

Collective biography, as well as individual biography, is part of
the literature of Anglican spirituality. Anglican religious communities have contributed much to the developing and shaping of
Anglican spirituality and to exemplifying the living out of that
spirituality in daily life. An early example of this kind of religious
community was the one founded in seventeenth century England
by Nicholas Ferrar (1593-1637), A. L. Maycock, *Nicholas Ferrar
and Little Gidding* (London: SPCK, 1938) is an account of it. In
the nineteenth century, the catholic revival gave rise to the
founding of a variety of religious communities in Anglicanism, the
Society of St. Margaret and the Society of St. John the Evangelist
(Cowley Fathers) being two examples. The record of their
corporate lives is illustrative of the impact of Anglican spirituality
upon life in the world.

Where does one find the literature of Anglican spirituality? The
literature of Anglican spirituality is where you find it. In collections
of prayers and in devotional aids, of course, and in the other
categories above, as well as in novels—Charles Williams (1886-
1947) is a case in point—and in plays—Dorothy Sayres' (1893-
1957) series *The Man Born to be King* being but one of many.

The temptation will be to indulge in the exercise of Anglican
triumphalism, seizing upon and cherishing a work expressly
because it is by or about an Anglican. If one seeks to find Anglican
spiritual literature—and there is nothing categorically wrong in
understaking that pursuit—the criterion cannot be simply in what
parish register the writer's baptism is recorded but the criteria of
consonance with the *Book of Common Prayer* and dynamic
relationship to daily living. In the total economy of Christian spirituality, these last are what Anglicans have to offer and to share.

Additional Resources

In addition to the books by Thornton and Stranks mentioned
above, the following books about Anglican spirituality may be of

interest to the reader. *History of Christian Spirituality* (London: Burns & Oates, 1968-1969) edited by Louis Bouyer, includes in its second volume a treatment of Anglican spirituality. John E. Booty in *Three Anglican Divines on Prayer* (Cambridge, Mass: Society of St. John the Evangelist, 1978) discusses three seventeenth century Anglicans: John Jewel, Lancelot Andrewes and Richard Hooker. *Spirituality for Today* (London: SCM, 1968), edited by Eric James, is a collection of papers and addresses presented to a conference of the Parish and People Movement in 1967. Helen C. White, a scholar of English literature, wrote extensively on devotional literature. Two of her works pertinent to this discussion are *Tudor Books of Private Devotion* (Madison: University of Wisconsin, 1951) and *English Devotional Literature (Prose) 1600-1640* (Madison: University of Wisconsin, 1931; reprinted 1966). Finally, a collection of essays published under the title *The Beauty of Holiness* (Oxford: SLG Press, 1976) is an introduction to six seventeenth century Anglicans: William Laud, Lancelot Andrewes, Jeremy Taylor, Mark Frank, George Herbert and Henry Vaughan.

ORDER THIS BOOK

Footnotes

[1] Henry VIII, Edward VI, and Elizabeth I each issued (in 1545, 1553 and 1559, respectively) an authorized primer, a small, vernacular prayer book.

[2] The term is used to designate a group of seventeenth century poets. In addition to John Donne and George Herbert, the poets customarily included in the term are Richard Crashaw (1612-1631), Henry Vaughan (1622-1695) and Thomas Traherne (1638-1674).

[3] "The Clapham Sect" was an informal association of Anglican Evangelicals of the parish of Clapham committed to a program of social and political reform in England.

III

Contrition in Anglican Spirituality: Hooker, Donne and Herbert

John E. Booty

That contrition is of considerable importance in Anglican spirituality is clearly evident in the theological writings, poetry and works of devotion by such exemplary divines of the sixteenth and seventeenth centuries as Hooker, Donne and Herbert. It is questionable, however, whether contrition is central in Anglicanism now. The *Book of Common Prayer*, that well-spring and guide for the formulators of early Anglican spirituality, has been criticized for its penitential emphasis. The General Confession has been faulted for its excessive language: "Phrases especially criticized are 'Provoking most justly thy wrath and indignation against us,' and 'The remembrance of them is grevious unto us; The burden of them is intolerable.' "[1] The 1928 revision of the Penitential Office was hailed as "liberating this telling act of penitence from morbid preoccupations with a supposed vitiation of human nature or futile luxury of grief over an irrevocable past."[2] The trend in more recent revisions has been toward making General Confession optional, placing greater emphasis on the eucharistic character of public worship, and generally making both private and public devotions happier, less excruciating experiences. The criticism indicates the possibility that we do not understand what was meant by contrition in the sixteenth century and that the *Book of Common Prayer* as devised then no longer conveys its original meaning. We shall consider what contrition meant to three early Anglicans, interpreters of the Prayer Book and representatives of spirituality of the age. Hooker, Donne and Herbert were champions of the great doctrine of contrition. To speak thus however, is, as we shall see, to speak of something broader than contrition alone for contrition in Anglican spirituality is intimately tied to the "sacrifice of praise and thanksgiving."

Hooker

Richard Hooker (1554-1600) was the first great theologian of Anglican tradition. In *Of the Laws of Ecclesiastical Polity* he not only defended the Elizabethan Settlement against Puritan objections; he interpreted the *Book of Common Prayer* to future generations and thus contributed to the formulation of Anglican spirituality. Book V of the *Laws* constitutes the heart and soul of his theological understanding as expressed in relation to the Prayer Book.[3] But that book should not be read alone. It depends upon the groundwork laid down in Books I-IV and on the further explication found in Books VI-VIII. Here Book VI should concern us most, for in it we have his most explicit and detailed discussion of contrition. Some have doubted that what we have is actually Book VI, and we must remember that it was not published until 1648, but there can be no doubt that it is Hooker's and that it is related by structure and meaning to Book V.[4]

What then is Hooker's doctrine? To begin we must see how Hooker answers the question, "What is the aim of life?" It is participation in God through Christ by the Holy Spirit, in the Church. This participation is achieved or, more properly, its achievement is acknowledged in various ways but principally in terms of creation and redemption. In terms of creation Hooker says, "God hath his influence into the verie essence of all thinges, without which influence of deitie supportinge them theire utter annihilation could not choose but followe (V.56.5).[5] In terms of redemption, we are in Adam, corrupt partakers of sin and death: we are in Christ, the Second Adam, and he in us, and thereby we possess his Spirit (V.56.7), freed from bondage to sin and death." Hooker makes it clear that the initiative rests with God and thus, in one place, he writes of Christ:

It pleaseth him in mercie to accompt him selfe incomplete and maimed without us.[6] But most assured wee are that wee all receave of his fulnes, because he is in us as a movinge and workinge cause, from which manie blessed effectes are reallie founde to ensue, and that in sundrie both kindes and degrees all tendinge to eternall happines (V.56.10).

Finally, through this work of the Spirit the Church, the body of Christ, is created and eternally recreated. To be in Christ is to be the Church. Indeed, this communion with the divine is the *ger-*

manissimam societatem, the seed of society (V.56.8); "they which belonge to the mysticall bodie of our Savior Christ . . . are . . . coupled everie one to Christ theire head and all unto everie particular person amongst them selves" (V.56.11). The sacraments he then views as instrumental in effecting the saving participation and thus in achieving the end or purpose of human existence.[7]

It is in relation to this statement of the goal of life as salvation from sin through participation in Christ that Hooker's understanding of contrition and the larger subject of repentance in Book VI should be understood, for we are here dealing with matters of ultimate importance for the Christian, the Church and the world, and not with an isolated problem of concern to the individual and no one else.

To begin with, Hooker is expounding a traditional doctrine. Repentance, or penitence as he sometimes calls it, involves, so Hooker says following the tradition, (1) "the aversion of the will from sin"; (2) "submission of ourselves to God by supplication and prayer"; and (3) "the purpose of a new life, testified with present works of amendment": or, in other words, contrition, confession, and satisfaction (VI.3.5).[8] For Hooker that which is most important to work our reconciliation with God "is the inward secret repentance of the heart." Thus, contrition comes first and is all important. But, if the sin confessed "be a crime injurious to" others, then "the wholesome discipline of God's Church exacteth a more exemplary and open satisfaction" (VI.3.1).

The beginning of repentance, then, is contrition. And in the beginning there is God's grace arousing contrition. "Which grace continually offereth itself, even unto them that have forsaken it, as may appear by the words of Christ in St. John's Revelation, 'I stand at the door and knock:' nor doth he only knock without, but also within assist to open" (VI.3.2). By grace the eye of faith is illuminated so that we meditate[9] upon "the resurrection of the dead, the judgment of the world to come, and the endless misery of sinners" (Ibid.). This meditation stimulates fear, which although it be "impotent and unable to advise itself; yet this good it hath, that men are thereby made desirous to prevent, if possibly they may, whatsoever evil they dread" (Ibid.). In this meditation the divine is pictured as the God of wrath, seeking revenge and punishment of those who sin. Hooker realizes the inadequacy of such a depiction, however, for he adds: "Howbeit, when faith hath wrought a fear of the event of sin, yet repentance hereupon ensueth not, unless our belief conceive both the possibility and means to avert evil: the possibility inasmuch as God is merciful, and most willing to have sin cured; the means, because he hath plainly taught what is requisite and shall suffice unto that purpose" (VI.3.3). Lacking this assurance, our human response to God's wrath results in attempts to suppress our fear and to obliterate our perception of God. Thus, "fear worketh no man's inclination to repentance, till some what else have wrought in us love also. Our love and desire of union with God ariseth from the strong conceit which we have of his admirable goodness. The goodness of God which particularly moveth unto repentance, is his mercy towards mankind, notwithstanding sin: for let it once sink deeply into the mind of man, that howsoever we have injuried God, his very nature is averse from revenge, except unto sin we add obstinacy" (Ibid.). The ultimate nature of God is revealed in mercy.

It is this simultaneous working of both fear and love toward God which is the work of faith, with love overwhelming fear, that sets the stage for contrition. Contrition he views as an inward grief, "a pensive and corrosive desire that we had done otherwise" than we have done in our sinfulness. Hooker put it this way:

> From these considerations, setting before our eyes our inexcusable both unthankfulness in disobeying so merciful, and foolishness in provoking so powerful a God, there ariseth necessarily a pensive and corrosive desire that we had done otherwise; a desire which suffereth us to foreslow no time, to feel no quietness within ourselves, to take neither sleep nor food with contentment, never to give over supplications, confessions, and other penitent duties, till the light of God's reconciled favour shine in our darkened soul" (VI.3.4).

Contrition in this understanding is a deeply felt affection, and certainly no shallow or routine thing. As Hooker says: "repentance must begin with a just sorrow, a sorrow of heart, and such a sorrow as renteth the heart; neither a feigned nor a slight sorrow; not feigned, lest it increase sin; nor slight, lest the pleasures of sin overmatch it" (VI.3.5).

The danger in such contrition is that of over-scrupulosity. Hooker is aware of this and toward the end of his treatise on repentance writes:

> Now there are . . . others, who doubting not of God's mercy toward all that perfectly repent, remain notwithstanding scrupulous

and troubled with continual fear, lest defects in their own repentance be a bar against them. These cast themselves first into very great, and peradventure needless agonies, through misconstruction of things spoken about proportioning our griefs to our sins, for which they never think they have wept and mourned enough; yea, if they have not always a stream of tears at commandment, they take it for a sign of a heart congealed and hardened in sin; when to keep the wound of contrition bleeding, they unfold the circumstances of their transgressions, and endeavour to leave out nothing which may be heavy against themselves. Yet do what they can, they are still fearful, lest herein also they do not that which they ought and might" (VI.6.17).

It seems that Hooker has in mind the second exhortation of the 1559 *Book of Common Prayer* which provides that if a person is unable to quiet his or her conscience "then let him come to me, or some other discreet and learned Minister of God's word, and open his grief, that he may receive such ghostly counsel, advice, and comfort, as his conscience may be relieved."[10] This is apparent as Hooker states that to aid the overly scrupulous, God in his mercy has ordained "consecrated persons, which by sentence of power and authority given from above, may as it were out of his very mouth ascertain timorous and doubtful minds in their own particular, ease them of all their scrupulosities, leave them settled in peace and satisfied touching the mercy of God towards them" (Ibid).[11]

In the end, then, it is the mercy of God, the divine love extended toward sinners, stimulating their response to that love which is the ground and heart of contrition and repentance. Contrition is aroused by God's love bringing forth a life—changing response of love in return. Hooker sees this most vividly in the sacraments, and in particular in the Eucharist, where there is not only the possibility but also the means for repentance, that is, for participation in Christ. For in a very real sense, to receive Christ in the sacrament is to receive God's love, to repent and to be forgiven, and to be renewed for lives of service. Commenting on I Cor. 10:16, Hooker writes:

Is there any thinge more expedite cleere and easie then that as Christ is termed our life because through him wee obteine life, so the partes of this sacrament are his bodie and blood for that they are so to us who receivinge them receive that by them which they are termed? The bread and cup are his bodie and blood because they are causes instrumentall upon the receipt whereof the *participation* of his bodie and bloode ensueth (V.67.5).

Donne

John Donne's understanding of the centrality of contrition for the Christian life is revealed in his *Devotions Upon Emergent Occasions* and by his Holy Sonnets. The *Devotions* were published in 1624 and concern a time when the Dean of St. Paul's suffered from some physical illness. Donne used the occasion to meditate upon his spiritual condition and to pray. Thus, paralleling the progress of his illness and recovery there is an equally serious consideration of his soul's health. As Gerard H. Cox III has pointed out, this meditation on his soul's health follows the course of repentance and is in many ways reminiscent of Hooker's description of that course.[12] The key-note is struck in Prayer I:

> enable me by thy grace to look forward to mine end, and to look backward too, to the considerations of thy mercies afforded me from the beginning; that so by that practice of considering thy mercy, in my beginning in this world, when thou plantedst me in the Christian church, and thy mercy in the beginning in the other world, when thou writest me in the book of life, in my election, I may come to a holy consideration of thy mercy in the beginning of all my actions here.[13]

The eye of faith being opened to behold the mercy of God, Donne then proceeds to that level called by Hooker the stimulation of fear. As the physician arrives, the sick man is afraid.[14] In Prayer VI we read: "O most mighty God, and merciful God, the God of all true sorrow, and true joy too, as thou hast given me a repentance, not to be repented of, so give me, O Lord, a fear, of which I may not be afraid."[15] It is noteworthy that the prayer for fear arises in the context of God's love. For Donne, God is goodness and love: "O eternal and most gracious God, who though thou have reserved thy treasure of perfect joy and perfect glory to be given by thine own hands then, when, by seeing thee as thou art in thyself, and knowing thee as we are known, we shall possess in an instant, and possess for ever, all that can any way conduce to our happiness . . ." The poet recites the blessings that come from God: "Nature reaches out her hand and gives us corn, and wine, and oil, and milk; but thou fillest her hand before, and thou openest her hand that she may rain down her showers upon us." And so he goes on until, in the end of Prayer VIII he beseeches God to be the physician of his soul in its distress.[16] With faith, love and fear, Donne confesses, recognizing that the persons of the Trinity are meeting to decide what shall be done "with this leprous soul."

> I offer not to counsel them who meet in consultation for my body now, but I open my infirmities, I anatomize my body to them. So I do my soul to thee, O my God, in an humble confession, that there is no vein in me that is not full of the blood of thy Son, whom I have crucified and crucified again, by multiplying many, and often repeating the same sins; that there is no artery in me that hath not the spirit of error, the spirit of lust, the spirit of giddiness in it; no bone in me that is not hardened with the custom of sin and nourished and suppled with the marrow of sin; no sinews, no ligaments, that do not tie and chain sin and sin together.[17]

But again, and immediately following this confession, Donne acknowledges God's love and mercy: "if you take this confession into a consultation, my case is not desperate, my destruction is not decreed." The "pensive and corrosive desire" is met by forgiveness and renewal.

The *Devotions* proceed; indeed, having gone this far we have not gone half way through them. Donne recognizes that his soul is still to some degree unrepentant, that there are yet sins hidden from God. He meditates on those last things identified by Hooker. He is preoccupied with death, his own death. He hears the church bells tolling for someone now dead and meditates on his connection to that dead one, his connection to all mankind:

> No man is an island entire of itself; every man is a piece of the continent, a part of the main. If a clod be washed away by the sea, Europe is the less, as well as if a promontory were, as well as if a manor of thy friend's or of thine own were: any man's death diminishes me, because I am involved in mankind, and therefore never send to know for whom the bell tolls; it tolls for thee.[18]

This fear of last things, and in particular of death, judgment and misery, has now, indeed, moved Donne's love for God.[19] The end and cure of body and soul is now in sight. Hope sustains the sinner and as the body is purged so is the soul purged by the working of God's spirit. Once more, through contrition, we arrive at confession. This confession is well worth dwelling upon:

I am come, by thy goodness, to the use of thine ordinary means for
my body, to wash away those peccant humours that endangered it.
I have, O Lord, a river in my body, but a sea in my soul, and a sea
swollen into the depth of a deluge, above the sea. Thou hast raised
up certain hills in me heretofore, by which I might have stood safe
from these inundations of sin.

He names these hills, our natural faculties, education and the
church with its word and sacraments, its holy ordinances. God
has led him to the top of all these hills,

> but this deluge, this inundation, is got above all my hills; and I
> have sinned and sinned, and multiplied sin to sin, after all these
> thy assistances against sin, and where is there water enough to
> wash away this deluge? There is a red sea, greater than this ocean,
> and there is a little spring, through which this ocean may pour
> itself into that red sea. Let thy spirit of true contrition and sorrow
> pass all my sins, through these eyes, into the wounds of thy Son,
> and I shall be clean, and my soul so much better purged than my
> body, as it is ordained for better and a longer life.[20]

The purgation of the soul begins with confession, proceeds to
mundare (the cleansing and purifying of the conscience by
detestation of sins),[21] and ends with *succidere*, to cut down and
weed out whatsoever remains that is unjustly procured by
restitution.[22] At the end of the *Devotions* there is an awareness of
the danger of relapse, physically and spiritually.[23] As Hooker put
it, "He which by repentance for sins had a purpose to satisfy the
Lord, will now by repenting his repentance make Satan
Satisfaction" (VI.5.1). It remains to say that Donne was aware of
the sin of over-scrupulosity, as was Hooker, and at the beginning
of his *Devotions* prayed to be delivered from vain imaginations of
sin: "that is an over-curious thing, a dangerous thing, to come to
that tenderness, that rawness, that scrupulousness, to fear every
concupiscence, every offer of sin, that this suspicious and jealous
diligence will turn to an inordinate dejection of spirit, and a
diffidence in thy care and providence."[24] In the beginning and in
the end there is God's love and mercy.[25]

Donne's justly famed Holy Sonnets have been interpreted by
Douglas L. Peterson as sonnets of contrition.[26] In so doing,
Peterson relies heavily on Hooker's dissertation on repentance
and to a very large extent makes a convincing case. The 1633
sequence of the sonnets as established by Helen Gardner,[27] is

composed of six sonnets concerned for the stimulation of fear and six concerned for the stimulation of love. Here are meditations on the last things, on death and resurrection, on judgment, and on the misery of the sinner. The first sonnet ("As due by many titles I resigne") is a kind of preparatory prayer, but with "O my blacke Soule! now thou art summoned" we have arrived at the contemplation of that which most arouses fear. The poet contemplates his death: "and I shall sleepe a space,/ But my'ever-waking part shall see that face,/ Whose feare already shakes my every joynt". The judgement is depicted and repentance yearned for in "At the round earths imagin'd corners, blow". The next sonnet reflects upon the transcendence of fear through love and is worth particular attention as transitional in nature. It expresses Hooker's understanding.

> *If poysonous mineralls, and if that tree,*
> *Whose fruit threw death on else immortall us,*
> *If lecherous goats, if serpents envious*
> *Cannot be damn'd; Alas; why should I bee?*
> *Why should intent or reason, borne in mee,*
> *Make sinnes, else equall, in mee, more heinous?*
> *And mercy being easie, and glorious*
> *To God, in his sterne wrath, why threatens hee?*
> *But who am I, that dare dispute with thee?*
> *O God, Oh! of thine onely worthy blood,*
> *And my teares, make a heavenly Lethean flood,*
> *And drown in it my sinnes blacke memorie.*
> *That thou remember them, some claime as debt,*
> *I thinke it mercy, if thou wilt forget.*

We cannot here consider the many dimensions of this rich poem. It is based upon Donne's conviction, over against the views of some Calvinists, that God is merciful, that blood and tears do indeed drown out human sins, and that God does forget them. "Death be not proud" is a magnificent expression of defiant faith in the face of prideful death, marking the end of those sonnets dealing with the stimulation of fear.

Those which concern the stimulation of love begin with meditations on the Cross of Christ in the Ignatian manner.[28] "Spit in my face" ends: "God cloth'd himselfe in vile mans flesh, that so/ Hee might be weake enough to suffer woe." "Why are wee by

all creatures waited on?" ends with amazement that the Creator
"whom sin, nor nature tyed,/ For us, his Creatures, and his foes,
hath dyed." "What if this present were the worlds last night?" goes
on to meditate:

> Marke in my heart, O Soule, where thou dost dwell,
> The picture of Christ crucified, and tell
> Whether that countenance can thee affright,
> Teares in his eyes quench the amasing light,
> Blood fills his frownes, which from his pierc'd head fell,
> And can that tongue adjudge thee unto hell,
> Which pray'd forgiveness for his foes fierce spight?

The next sonnet, "Batter my heart, three person'd God," in
frankly sexual terms,[29] reflects the struggles of one who would
repent but is unable unless the almighty and merciful God act to
free him from his sin. The poet cries out:

> Divorce mee, 'untie, or breake that knot againe,
> Take mee to you, imprison mee, for I
> Except you'enthrall mee, never shall be free,
> Nor ever chast, except you ravish mee.

"Wilt thou love God, as he thee" returns to the meditative mood
to remember God's adoption of humankind to reign together with
the Creator and Ruler of all. The final sonnet, "Father, part of his
double interest," ends with a clear and firm evocation of the divine
Love. He meditates upon the Law and the Gospel, the laws of the
old dispensation which none fulfill and the law of the new which
fulfills all.

> . . . but thy all-healing grace and Spirit,
> Revive againe what law and letter kill.
> Thy lawes abridgement, and thy last command
> Is all but love; Oh let that last Will stand!

These sonnets were written by one who was struggling for faith,
for true contrition, and for newness of life. At times he seemed to
be struggling against God, and yet in each he speaks to and with
God in ways which indicate his trust. The eyes of faith have been
opened and he perceives the ultimate truth, that God is merciful,

that God loves his creatures, and that God is crucified again and again, sorrowing on account of human sin.
The 1635 sequence of sonnets expresses contrite sorrow.[30] They are expressive of that pensive and corrosive desire to which Hooker referred. They also express that mutual love of God and the poet which is fundamental to Donne's understanding of the Christian life. None of the four is more impressive than the first.

Thou hast made me, And shall thy worke decay?
Repaire me now, for now mine end doth haste,
I runne to death, and death meets me as fast,
And all my pleasures are like yesterday,
I dare not move my dimme eyes any way,
Despaire behind, and death before doth cast
Such terrour, and my febled flesh doth waste
By sinne in it, which it t'wards hell doth weigh;
Onely thou art above, and when towards thee
By thy leave I can looke, I rise againe;
But our old subtle foe so tempteth me,
That not one houre I can my selfe, sustaine;
Thy Grace may wing me to prevent his art
And thou like Adamant draw mine iron heart.

It would not be incorrect to refer to the theology of John Donne as the theology of divine mercy. "His most constant biblical theme [in his sermons] is the mercy of God, and the words most frequently quoted are those of the psalmist, 'His mercy is over all his works.' "[31] Thus, in spite of the persistent penitential tone of his *Devotions* and his Holy Sonnets the focus is not on sin but on love, God's forgiving love arousing the response of love. It is with conviction that at the end of his *Essays in Divinity* he prays:

O Eternal and most merciful God, against whom, as we know and acknowledge that we have multiplied contemptuous and rebellious sins, so we know and acknowledg too, that it were a more sinfull contempt and rebellion, then all those, to doubt of thy mercy for them . . .[32]

3. The Altar.

A BROKEN ALTAR, Lord, thy fervant rears,
Made of a heart, and cemented with tears :
Whofe parts are as thy hand did frame ;
No workman's tool hath touch'd the fame.
   A HEART alone
   Is fuch a ftone,
   As nothing but
   Thy power doth cut.
   Wherefore each part
   Of my hard heart
   Meets in this frame,
   To praife thy name :
That, if I chance to hold my peace,
Thefe ftones to praife thee may not ceafe.
O let thy bleffed SACRIFICE be mine,
And fanctify this ALTAR to be thine.

Herbert

George Herbert (1593-1633), the priest and poet, was sensitively aware of the vital importance of contrition to Anglican
spirituality, and to the Christian life wherever and whenever it
might be. There is no greater proof of this than is to be found in
that sequence of poems which was published posthumously and
called *The Temple*. Like the *Book of Common Prayer*, which
influenced it,[33] *The Temple* moves from contrition to praise and is
imbued with contrition in all its parts. The first poems of the work,
from "The Church Porch" through "H. Baptisme II" represent the
entrance into the Church building and into the Christian life. We
begin in "The Church Porch" with a kind of Catechism which is
also a self-examination organized around a consideration of the
seven deadly sins and their corresponding virtues. It is subtitled
"Perirrhanterium," a Greek term, *aspergillum* in Latin, referring to
an instrument used for sprinkling holy water. Herbert had in mind

the *asperges* (derived from Ps. 50:9 in the Vulgate: "Thou shalt sprinkle me with hyssop and I shall be cleansed: thou shalt wash me and I shall be whiter than snow") symbolizing cleansing and bringing to mind Baptism. The self-examination, which ends with the "Superliminare" is the necessary exercise for one who would enter the church, approach the holy, praise and glorify God.

When the door opens, Herbert sees the altar and in a remarkable pattern poem, shaped like an altar, experiences, by a process of *metataxis*,[34] a kind of elevation beyond the physical reality into a spiritual sphere. The self-examination which was a preparatory exercise involving largely the mind now yields to the experience of contrition. One must note, however, that the experience occurs within the context of God's love shown forth in the sacrifice of the Lord. Furthermore, close inspection reveals that the visual impact of the poem is one of stasis, solidity, with lines of equal length in couplets. The eye begins at the altar or table top and descends, drawing in as the pillar conjoining the top to the base emerges. The sound of the words and lines conforms to the visual image. The lines in the pillar section are sharp, abrupt, ending "but . . . cup" and "part . . . heart." This was all carefully planned by the poet to move the reader from contrition to praise. We see, we approach the altar and in the light of it we know that what we have to present is not perfect and whole, but something flawed and broken. *Metataxis* is immediately at work, for the stone altar standing in the sanctuary becomes my heart, a broken altar, held together, cemented by tears of contrition. This heart, Lord, is as you made it, no other workman contributed anything to it. This second couplet is both an explanation and a cry from the broken heart. As we move into the pillar we descend into hell. Such a heart as mine is as stone — hard, impenetrable, cold — which nothing can cut, nothing can break to make it in contrition that which God means it to be. With the end of the first two couplets of the pillar we are at the center of the poem. We then descend to a deeper level (and our spirits begin to rise) for with God's power "each part/ Of my hard heart/ Meets in this frame,/ To praise thy name." That is to say, God does work on our hearts by the power of the Holy Spirit to make them contrite and thus able to love God and worship in spirit and in truth. Now the lines spread out as the thought expands. Thus, if we do not resist, but let God work in and on us, "These stones to praise thee may not cease." The final couplet yields the final, deepest thought, which is a prayer and a song of praise, leading us to the next poem. "O let thy blessed Sacrifice be mine,/ And sanctifie this Altar to be thine." The poem moves from the lesser to the greater, from the altar as mere stone, to the altar of the heart, and from thence to the altar of the Cross and we know that it is in the light of the latter that both of the former are to be understood. Indeed, the sacrifice of Christ on the Cross makes possible the sacrifice of praise and thanksgiving.

"The Sacrifice" is a kind of liturgy, influenced by the medieval Improperia and Reproaches of Good Friday. The contritional nature of it is revealed in the first stanza. Christ is speaking to us:

> Oh all ye, who passe by, whose eyes and minde
> To worldly things are sharp, but to me blinde;
> To me, who took eyes that I might you finde:
> Was ever grief like mine?

Here we have a lengthy, detailed meditation on the Passion and on one's life in relation to it. The divine sorrow elicits human contrition. We are also made aware, in the end, of the necessity of this sacrifice for our salvation, an awareness which elicits the sacrifice of praise and thanksgiving. "For they will pierce my side, I full well know;/ That as sinne came, so Sacraments might flow."

Contrition is dominant in the poems that follow. In "Thanksgiving" the poet strives to make some appropriate response to Christ's sacrifice, but fails. In "The Reprisall" he acknowledges his failure. There is nothing he can do but repent:

> Yet by confession will I come
> Into thy conquest: though I can do nought
> Against thee, in thee I will overcome
> The man, who once against thee fought.

Herbert's struggle involves his constant desire to do something that will merit God's love. His constant task is to realize that the only thing he can do is to be contrite, open to the Lord's coming, fed by love. "The Agonie" ends:

> *Who knows not Love, let him assay*
> *And taste that juice, which on the crosse a pike*
> *Did set again abroach; then let him say*
> *If ever he did taste the like.*
> *Love is that liquor sweet and most divine,*
> *Which my God feels as bloud; but I, as wine.*

Here, as is so often the case, contrition becomes praise as the knowledge of God's love makes it possible by contrition for that love to be received.

At the end of this opening sequence, a kind of introduction for the entire work, the predominant note is that of praise, although with contrition evident as an element of that praise. Good Friday yields to Easter, condemnation to redemption, with the lyrical and lovely two part poem, "Easter." It begins:

> *Rise heart; thy Lord is risen. Sing his praise*
> *Without delayes,*
> *Who takes thee by the hand, that thou likewise*
> *With him mayst rise.*

The contrite, forgiven Christian is enjoined to break forth in song. The second part is the song of praise, tender and strong. But the first part is also a kind of song. In the first stanza there is praise for the one who by his death reduced us to dust, dust and ashes, contrition and confession; by his life, his risen triumphant life, he raises us making dust into "gold, and much more, just." In the second stanza the metaphor is musical. Christ on the Cross, stretched out, is the string who sounds the note appropriate to celebrate the Paschal feast.[35] In the third stanza, Herbert reflects on the fact that heart and lute require a third thing: the Holy Spirit.[36] True music, true harmony, requires such assistance to make the common chord; grace is needed if true harmony, the music of the spheres is to be reached.

"Easter-wings" is another pattern poem, relying on sight and sound for effect, imbued with contrition and praise, in each butterfly like stanza beginning with contrition.[37] The poet laments his lost of the gifts bestowed on humanity at creation and sings the praises of the Lord through whom the lost is recovered:

> *Lord, who createdst man in wealth and store,*
> *Though foolishly he lost the same,*
> *Decaying more and more,*
> *Till he became*
> *Most poore:*
> *With thee*
> *O let me rise*
> *As larks, harmoniously,*
> *And sing this day thy victories:*
> *Then shall the fall further the flight in me.*

> *My tender age in sorrow did beginne:*
> *And still with sicknesses and shame*
> *Thou didst so punnish sinne,*
> *That I became*
> *Most thinne.*
> *With thee*
> *Let me combine*
> *And feel this day thy victorie:*
> *For, if I imp my wing on thine,*
> *Affliction shall advance the flight in me.*

There is no denying the intensity of Herbert's contrition. It is surely as vivid as that expressed in the Elizabethan Prayer Book's General Confession. The poem "Repentance" begins,

> *Lord, I confesse my sinne is great;*
> *Great is my sinne.*

The emphasis increases as Herbert says:

> *O let thy height of mercie then*
> *Compassionate short-breathed men.*
> *Cut me not off for my most foul transgression:*
> *I do confesse*
> *My foolishnesse;*
> *My God, accept of my confession.*

He begs the Lord to "Sweeten at length this bitter bowl,/ Which thou hast pour'd into my soul; Thy wormwood turn to health."

The weight of sin, the self-hatred, the contrition are all things for which God is responsible, making the poet, woeful and wan, causing his heart to "Pine, and decay." But he ends with that which makes it possible to begin on this sorrowful road: God's merciful love.

> But thou wilt sinne and grief destroy;
> That so the broken bones may joy,
> And tune together in a well-set song,
> Full of his praises,
> Who dead men raises.
> Fractures well cur'd make us more strong.

That is to say that we might ignore our condition, our sinfulness, be happily engaged in our business, and know nothing of the pain of guilt. But God sent his Son to die on the Cross for us. Looking upon him, engaged in his passion, we are plunged into darkness. Guilt ridden, condemned, contrite, we are broken, as a broken stone or altar or bone. We acknowledge our true condition and are thereby made ready to receive the divine, healing, joyful love, for which we sing out praises.

The major section of *The Temple*, called "The Church," ends with one of Herbert's finest poems, "Love III." Here the Christian is welcomed to the banquet, the messianic banquet, the Lord's Supper, by the Lord, called "Love," and yet draws back, "Guiltie of dust and sinne." The Lord notices that the Christian is hanging back and asks if he lacks anything. "A guest, I answer'd, worthy to be here: / Love said, You shall be he." The Christian protests; unkind, ungrateful he cannot even look on the Lord. But the Lord takes his hand and asks "Who made the eyes but I?" The Christian acknowledges that this is true but protests again, saying, "but I have marr'd them" and asks that he be left to his just deserts. The Lord responds, "And know you not . . . who bore the blame?" The Christian surrenders, but not altogether, asserting himself as is his custom to do something meritorious. "My deare, then I will serve." But the Lord is firm, "You must sit down, sayes Love, and taste my meat," and the response is the only acceptable one, indicating the final end of contrition: "So I did sit and eat." We recall here Hooker's warning against over-scrupulosity. The feeling of unworthiness inhibits the poet's participation in the saving feast and in the new life in Christ. So too does the effort to maintain control over one's life and destiny, an effort which so often characterizes those who feel unworthy. To be a Christian means that one must accept the fact that by Christ's sacrifice the sinner has been made worthy. Now, at the last, the contrite, forgiven sinner is powerless to do anything but receive the Love which has cleansed and renewed him.

To a very considerable extent, Herbert in his own way reflects that understanding which we have already encountered in Hooker and in Donne.

Conclusion

Hooker, Donne and Herbert share a common understanding of contrition. The tradition they represent assumed that contrition is a fruit of the Gospel as it is preached and received. "God so loved the world that he gave his only Son, that whoever believes in him should not perish but have everlasting life" (John 3:16). The rood may have been removed, or it may not, but the sixteenth century Christian pictured Christ crucified, triumphant over sin and death. Beholding the love emanating from the blessed rood, the Christian felt judged, condemned, unworthy to receive such love. Contrition fills the soul and a yearning, "a pensive and corrosive desire that we had done otherwise" than we have done. In that dark moment, God seems to be wrathful, condemning the sinner to eternal damnation. But behind the wrath, piercing the darkness with light, love persists. The Christian contemplates the last things, assisted by visual and auditory representations. Death, judgment and endless misery become more and more vivid as they are contemplated and now contrition is infused with fear and holy dread. Still, in spite of all, love persists. We are at the point of extreme danger. We may yield to soul-destroying despair, we may wallow in our guilt, we may seek to suppress the fear and discard the "pensive and corrosive desire," turning away from love to embrace our loves. Or, we may struggle ever more fiercely to retain control of our lives and our destinies, to do that which merits the divine love, indeed coerces God to forgive us. This was Herbert's abiding temptation. But, by the persistence of love, steadfast, wholly unmerited, we turn, and in turning toward God as we are turned, we acknowledge that God through Christ makes us worthy, draws from us love, sacrificial love toward God and toward the world God made and redeems.

This does not mean that in a brief moment in time we repent for all of our lives and have no need for further repentance. Contrition is more than an isolated act of piety. Indeed it involves not only confession and absolution but newness of life. Contrition is fundamental to that worship of God which is a life long *latria*, service towards God, our neighbors, and the rest of creation. It involves that attitude towards the self that suppresses and hopefully will eliminate the sin of pride. When the altar of the heart is broken in contrition it is thereby opened, made available to the working of God's Spirit, open to faith, hope and love. The contrite heart, freed from the crippling preoccupation with the self's demands, is freed to see and to listen as only a very few seem able to see and listen. In contrition we can see, hear, touch, taste in a new and life-giving way. We can see beauty not as spectators but as participants for we are open to the creativity of that which is beautiful. We can hear the cries of the poor and the assurance of friends, for we are no longer listening to our own voices demand more and more of what we conceive to be our just rewards. We can touch and know that other beside us with a new sensitivity, for we are no longer fearful of contamination. We can taste the bread and wine as the Body and Blood of our Savior, for we are no longer preoccupied with satisfying our intellectual pride or with avoiding the embarrassment of belief in the presence of disbelieving friends. In short, the contrite person is the available person, available for participation in that which ultimately matters.

Contrition furthermore involves that *diakonia* which defines the people of God and in turn *diakonia* involves contrition, that attitude or frame of mind and heart and soul proper to those who acknowledge themselves to be forgiven sinners. Or, to put it another way, Jesus told his disciples that he came not to be served but to serve (Mark 10:45); he said, "I am among you as one who serves" (Luke 22:27). The church as the extension of Christ's ministry in time and space is defined not in terms of wealth, numbers, institutional power, or the like, but rather it is defined by the service it renders, by its self-giving for the sake of others, by sacrifice which Maurice identified as the law of humankind. Ambrose, the Bishop of Milan in the fourth century, put it succinctly: "The wealth of the Church is what it spends on the poor." If then the Church is *diakonia*, it is composed of those who are known for their contrition, for only those who are contrite, knowing their limitations and their sin, knowing too that they are forgiven by the servant Lord, and dedicated to the new life, which is the life of service, are fit and ready to be servants, to be the church as *diakonia*. To be a servant is a high calling, sometimes necessitating special skills, costly training, but we begin as servant by virtue of our contrition.

In some ways the problem of the church in this age is that it has forgotten its identity and is desperately attempting to be that which by nature it cannot be and still be the church. Its apostacy calls for contrition, that is for reformation and renewal as *diakonia*. If it does indeed recapture its identity, and there is no reason to believe that it cannot do so, for it is the temple of the Holy Spirit, that renewal will mark the beginning of a new and hopeful chapter in the church's history.

Contrition is thus necessary to the church and its mission and should be the keynote of our private and public devotions. This is said mindful of the fact that contrition is a beginning and not an end for true contrition issues in thanksgiving and praise. Contrition is also necessary to our world. The present escalating competition for the remaining, dwindling resources of planet earth—to name but one of the greatest crises we face and shall face for the forseeable future—will surely lead to war and such destruction as can hardly be imaged unless the nations and those that inhabit them adopt different attitudes from those that now preoccupy them. In place of competition there needs to be cooperation. In place of concern now only for our own comfort and convenience, there needs to be concern for the deprived and oppressed of the world and for future generations that inherit what we leave for them to inherit. In place of a fixation on continuous growth and expansion, we need to strive for a stable condition in which we strive only for that which is actually needed to sustain us. Such "deprivation" has potential to free us from the frenzy to attain that ever illusive better standard of life, to free us to enjoy the abundance that we have now, to enjoy it and to share it. Such a revolution in values and goals requires, I believe, people who live their lives in a state of grateful contrition, sensitive to the love of God, realistically aware of their shortcomings and limitations, and with the openness, availability that results in living by the Spirit, not by selfish, grasping spirits, being Christ's instruments in the world, people that live to serve others with a service that is truly sacrificial. This is what humanity is meant to be and to do. For this we were created; to this life of contrite service we were redeemed.

The hope of the world rests with the redemption of its inhabitants. Hooker, Donne and Herbert lived in an age now past with a world view that differs greatly from ours, but they can help us to understand the importance of contrition in Anglican spirituality and in humanity at large. In doing so they are helping us to understand something deeply true about Christianity and its message and mission in the present age. Above all, they affirm that true praise, joy and thanksgiving proceed out of that contrition which is the gift of divine love. This is the message of Herbert's "Praise II":

> King of Glorie, King of Peace,
>   I will love thee:
> And that love may never cease,
>   I will move thee.
> Thou hast granted my request,
>   Thou hast heard me:
> Thou didst note my working breast,
>   Thou hast spared me.
> Wherefore with my utmost art
>   I will sing thee.

> And the cream of all my heart
>   I will bring thee.
> Though my sinnes against me cried,
>   Thou didst cleare me;
> And alone, when they replied,
>   Thou didst heare me.
> Sev'n whole dayes, not one in seven,
>   I will praise thee.
> In my heart, though not in heaven,
>   I can raise thee.
> Thou grew'st soft and moist with tears,
>   Thou relentedst:
> And when Justice call'd for fears,
>   Thou dissentedst.
> Small it is, in this poore sort
>   To enroll thee:
> Ev'n eternitie is too short
>   To extoll thee.

Footnotes

[1] *The Standing Liturgical Commission, Prayer Book Studies IV: The Eucharistic Liturgy* (New York: Church Pension Fund, 1953), p. 231.

[2] Edward Lambe Parsons and Bayard Hale Jones, *The American Prayer Book: Its Origins and Principles* (New York: Charles Scribner's Sons, 1950), p. 148.

[3] For a description of Hooker's theology in relation to Book V, see my chapter in *The Spirit of Anglicanism*, William J. Wolf, ed. (Wilton, Conn.: Morehouse-Barlow, 1979), pp. 1-45.

[4] Concerning the authenticity of Book VI, see W. Speed Hill, "Hooker's *Polity*, The Problem of the 'Three Last Books,' " *Huntington Library Quarterly*, 34(4), August 1971, pp. 317-36. But see also A. S. McGrade, "Repentance and Spiritual Power: Book VI of Richard Hooker's *Of the Laws of Ecclesiastical Polity*," *Journal of Ecclesiastical History*, 29(2), April 1978, pp. 163-76, where a case is made for its authenticity as Book VI itself.

[5] Citations to Hooker's *Laws* are given in the text. The roman numeral stands for the book, the first arabic number for the chapter, and the second for the section. The text used for Book V is that of the Folger Shakespeare Library edition of Hooker's *Works*, Vol. 2, W. Speed Hill, ed. (Cambridge, Mass.: Harvard University Press, 1977). The text for Book VI is that of the *Works*, Vol. 3, Keble, Church, and Paget, eds. (Oxford: Clarendon Press, 1888).

[6] Hooker refers to Eph. 1:22-23 and evidently has in mind the marginal note in the Geneva Bible: "This is the great love of Christ towards his Church that he counteth not himself perfect without us which are his members . . ."

[7] On his view of the sacraments, see *Spirit of Anglicanism*, pp. 31-32, and Ronald Bayne in Hooker, *Of the Laws of Ecclesiastical Polity, The Fifth Book* (London: Macmillan, 1902), pp. cvii-cxx.

[8] Concerning the sacrament of penance see Thomas Acquinas, *S.T.*, 3a84-90; concerning contrition, see ibid., 3 suppl. 1-5; and see Booty, "Preparation for the Lord's Supper in Elizabethan England," *Anglican Theological Review* XLIX(2), April 1967, pp. 131-148.

[9] Concerning the importance of the meditative tradition as derived from the *Scala Meditatoria* see Louis Martz, *The Poetry of Meditation* (New Haven: Yale University Press, 1954).

[10] *The Book of Common Prayer, 1559*, ed. J. Booty (Charlottesville, Va.: University of Virginia Press, 1976), p. 257.

[11] Concerning Hooker's understanding of the power and authority of clergy in relation to absolution, see *Laws*, V.77.1,5-7.

[12] "Donne's *Devotions*: A Meditative Sequence on Repentance," *Harvard Theological Review*, 66, 1973, pp. 331-351.

[13] Donne, *Devotions Upon Emergent Occasions, Together with Death's Duel* (Ann Arbor, Mich.: University of Michigan Press, 1959), p. 11.

[14] Ibid., pp. 35-36.

[15] Ibid., pp. 41-42.

[16] Ibid., p. 56.

[17] Ibid., p. 60, Expostulation IX.

[18] Ibid., pp. 108-109, Meditation XVII.

[19] Ibid., pp. 120-121, Prayer XVIII.

[20] Ibid., pp. 137-138, Prayer XX.

[21] Ibid., pp. 138-145.

[22] Ibid., pp. 152-160.

[23] Ibid., pp. 159-160, Prayer XXIII.

[24] Ibid., p. 11, Prayer I.

[25] For another interpretation in the modern mode, see D. W. Harding, "The *Devotions* Now," in *John Donne: Essays in Celebration*, ed. A. G. Smith (London: Methuen, 1972), pp. 385-403.

[26] *The English Lyric* (Princeton: Princeton University Press, 1967), pp. 330-348. I am much indebted to this discussion.

[27] See Donne, *Divine Poems*, ed. Helen Gardner (Oxford: Clarendon Press, 1953). The poems as arranged by Gardner can be viewed thusly:

1633 sequence
Stimulation of fear
1. As due by many titles I resign
2. Oh my blacke Soule
3. This is my playes last scene
4. At the round earths imagin'd corners
5. If poysonous mineralls
6. Death be not proud
Stimulation of love
1. Spit in my face yee Jewes
2. Why are wee by all creatures
3. What if this present
4. Batter my heart
5. Wilt thou love God
6. Father, part of his double interest

[28] See Martz, *Poetry of Meditation*, pp. 43-56, and Gardner's intro. to the *Divine Poems*.

[29] Concerning the sexual imagery in Donne's poems, see Murray Rosten, *The Soul of Wit: A Study of John Donne* (Oxford: Clarendon Press, 1974), pp. 174-179.

[30] Thus Peterson, *English Lyric*, p. 335.

[31] A. C. Sculpholme, "Anniversary Study of John Donne. Pt. 2. Fraited with Salvation," *Theology*, 75, 1972, pp. 75-76.

[32] Donne, *Essays in Divinity*, ed. Evelyn M. Simpson (Oxford: At the Clarendon Press, 1952), p. 99.

[33] See my article, "George Herbert: *The Temple* and the *Book of Common Prayer*," *Mosaic*, XII/2, Winter 1979, pp. 75-90.

[34] See Dick Higgins, *George Herbert's Pattern Poems: In their Tradition* (West Glover, Vermont and New York: 1977).

[35] See Donne's sermon on Ezek. 33:32 (*Sermons*, ed. G. R. Potter and E. M. Simpson, Berkeley and Los Angeles: University of Chicago Press, 1953-1962, II:170) where, on account of the discord brought about by the Fall, "God had rectified all again, by putting in a new string, *semen mulieris*, the seed of woman, the *Messias*: And onely by sounding that string in your ears, become we *musicum carmen*, true music, true harmony, true peace to you."

[36] See F. E. Hutchinson, ed., *The Works of George Herbert* (Oxford: Clarendon Press, 1941), pp. 489-490.

[37] See Higgins, *George Herbert's Pattern Poems*, p. 16, and Joseph Summers, *George Herbert: His Religion and Art* (Cambridge, Mass.: Harvard University Press, 1954), p. 144.

IV

The Spirituality
of
Thomas Traherne

William J. Wolf

Since the rediscovery of Thomas Traherne at the beginning of this century, he has fascinated literary critics and devotional readers alike. The cadences of that day's *Book of Common Prayer* are his warp and woof. The flexibility of his sentences and the rhythmic chanting of his prose in his exultant *Thanksgivings* have been compared with Walt Whitman's *Leaves of Grass*. In his poetry and in his prose which is often more poetical than his poetry there are uncanny anticipations of Wordsworth and Blake: "You never Enjoy the World aright, till you see how a Sand Exhibiteth the Wisdom and Power of God" (I,27) finds its parallel in Blake's "to see a world in a grain of sand."[1]

Gladys Wade, Traherne's biographer, claims that had he written nothing more than the third meditation in the "Third Centurie" he, ". . . would stand among the great masters of English prose."[2] Her judgment, while that of an enthusiast, is hardly too strong if we consider the excellence of the passage. Traherne's words have a mysteriously suggestive power to evoke our admiration and to give us the conviction that these words are just the ones required to reveal the eternal in the common things of everyday. Through Traherne we are led to see that only the childlike spirit can perceive reality in its depth. The gospel admonition that we must become like little children to enter the Kingdom of God is illuminated for us.

"The Corn was Orient and Immortal Wheat, which never should be reaped, nor was ever sown. I thought it had stood from everlasting to everlasting. The Dust and Stones of the Street were as Precious as GOLD. The Gates were at first the End of the World. The Green Trees when I saw them first through one of the Gates Transported and Ravished me: their Sweetnes and unusual

Beauty made my Heart to leap, and almost mad with Extasie . . ."
The effect of his words is greatly aided by a rolling rhythm that
suggests the ebb and flow of wind-blown waves of wheat. Later in
the same meditation, he confesses: "So that with much adoe I
was corrupted: and made to learn the Dirty Devices of this World.
Which now I unlearn, and becom as it were a little Child again,
that I may enter into the Kingdom of GOD" (III,3). The reader
senses Traherne's credibility and opens himself expecting authentic teaching about the meaning of our life.

Traherne's prose leads to the appreciation of the beauty of
holiness. When his *Centuries of Meditations* so recently found in
manuscript in a bookseller's stall, shall have worked themselves by
use into the heart of Western devotion, they may well displace in
popularity Thomas à Kempis *Imitation of Christ*. The latter's is a
monkish piety seeking the salvation of its own soul, while
Traherne's devotion is meant for the person of affairs and seeks
the salvation of the whole world. The son of Bertram Dobell, the
agnostic discoverer of Traherne, appreciated the religious depth
of what his father could only see as beauty: "No other work
written in the English language equals it as a Manual of Devotion.
No other work so beautifully extols the wonders of Divine Love,
and certainly no one can read Traherne's burning phrases without
being conscious of an enlargment of his vision . . . In the character
of Traherne the qualities of the Poet, the Mystic, and the Saint are
all found in a very high degree, if not indeed in their highest manifestations . . . He was not more a Poet than a Mystic, nor more a
Mystic than a Saint, but each at all times, and never one rather
than the other."[3] The last word about Traherne's style and accom-
plishments should go to a fellow poet, John Masefield: "He
comes to us in these latter days like the first of the larks in spring;
like a bright dawn coming suddenly above solemn hills."[4]

Traherne Rediscovered

Although Traherne's *Christian Ethicks* had enjoyed a modest
sale in its day, it and its author had long passed out of human
memory. Then in 1895 William Brooke, rummaging in a second
hand bookshop in London, found two manuscript volumes, one
of poetry and the other of meditations. The poems bore a
resemblance to the work of Henry Vaughan. Vaughan's editor
was about to incorporate them into his new edition when his

death prevented a serious miscarriage of scholarship. Bertram
Dobell, the friend of the poet James Thompson and a bookseller,
bought the manuscripts and after careful internal analysis convinced Brooke and others that they could not be Vaughan's.
Brooke then recalled using a joyous poem much like this poetry
from an anonymous book in the British Museum with the pon-
derous title *A Serious and Pathetical Contemplation of the
Mercies of God, in Several Most Devout and Sublime
Thanksgivings for the Same.* Search revealed a clue in the Preface
to the effect that the author had been "to the service of the late
Lord Keeper Bridgman as his chaplain." Further research established Traherne as Bridgman's chaplain, but conclusive identification was wanting until Dobell discovered casually recorded in
the prose of *Christian Ethicks* some poetry that was also in his
manuscript volume. Thus, by luck and some clever literary
sleuthing, Traherne was rediscovered. Dobell edited his poetry in
1903 and his *Centuries of Meditations* in 1908. (The significance
of the title is that Traherne numbered his paragraphs and when he
reached 101 chose to call it the first paragraph of the "Second
Centurie.")

Life and Writings

It may be said paradoxically that we know a great deal about
Thomas Traherne and that we really know very little. The external
facts are few, chiefly from parish registers, wills, prefaces, and
from Anthony à Woods' *Athenae Oxonienses*, a *Who's Who* of
Oxford men in the seventeenth century. The facts are few and the
chronology indefinite. Every careful reader, however, of the
Poems and *Centuries* would want to say that we know much
about Traherne the person from the autobiographical details
strewn like nuggets through his writings. His spirit, his disciplined
life, his intense recollection of his infancy, his joy and delight in
the world of nature and in the universe of words are all clearly
evident even though the biographer may despair of establishing
sequences and dates. Here is a slightly abbreviated version of
Wood, our best source.

"Thomas Traherne, a shoemaker's son of Hereford was
entered a commoner of Brase(nose) college on the first day of
March 1652, took one degree in arts, left the house for a time,
entered into the sacred function, and in 1661 he was actually

created master of arts. About that time he became rector of
Credenhill commonly called Crednell near to the city of Hereford,
afterwards domestic chaplain to S. Orlando Bridgman lord
Keeper of the great seal, and minister of Tuddington, called by
some Teddington, near Hampton Court in Middlesex, and in
1669 bach. of divinity. He hath written, *Roman Forgeries . . .
(and) Christian Ethics: or divine Morality, opening the Way to
Blessedness, by the Rules of Virtue and Reason . . .* He died at
Teddington before mentioned, in the house of S. Orl. Bridgman,
and was buried on the tenth of October in the church there, under
the reading desk, in sixteen hundred seventy and four. This
person, who always led a single and a devout life, was well read in
primitive antiquity as in the councils, fathers, etc."[5]

Thomas Traherne was born in 1637 into a family that suffered
from hard times and probably inner strife. Although Thomas
poured forth his thanksgivings articulately to God for all things
there is not to be found any word of gratitude for his parents' care.
Instead we find this: "it is not so much our Parents' Loyns, so
much as our Parents lives that Enthrals and Blinds us" (III, 8). As
a lad he questioned his fate: "how comes it to pass therefore that I
am so poor? of so Scanty and Narrow a fortune, enjoying few and
Obscure Comforts?" (III,16). His parents may have died when
Thomas and his brother Philip were quite young. They may have
been raised then in far better circumstances by a relative Philip
Traherne who kept an inn and was sometime mayor of Hereford.
Hereford, a walled-city in the west of England bordering on
Wales, was set in a beautiful countryside of woods, hills, clear
streams and orchards of Red Streak apples. This earthy paradise
that so transported the growing boy became a ravaged land
during the civil wars. It was plundered first by one side and then
by the other, even sustaining a six-week siege by the dreaded
Scottish army. Thomas would have been twenty three at the Restoration of Charles II. From his school days for a period that
cannot now be dated Thomas was consciously sceptical in matters
of faith: "How can I believ that He gave His Son to die for me,
who having Power to do otherwise gave me nothing but Rags?"
(II,6).

To Oxford

Brasenose was the most Puritan of the Oxford colleges.

Thomas, finding at last the Bible as a revelation addressed to his condition, studied it closely. He developed friendly relations with the Puritan clergy of Hereford who ordained him. These men were ejected at the Restoration, but Thomas received episcopal ordination apparently with little sense of crisis or acute transition. It is clear that he became a dedicated scholar at the university, laying the foundations for his later researches and original contributions in church history. "There I saw into the Nature of the Sea, the Heavens, the Sun, the Moon and Stars, the Elements, Minerals, and Vegetables. All which appeared like the King's daughter, All Glorious within" (III,36). These subjects were "Things which my Nurses and Parents should hav talkt of" (III,36). From the perspective of later years, however, he could write: "Nevertheless som things were Defectiv too. There was never a Tutor that did profesly Teach Felicity: tho that be the Mistress of all other Sciences . . .We Studied to inform our Knowledg, but Knew not for what End we so Studied" (III,37). (By "felicity" Traherne meant *happiness* or *blessedness*.)

To Credenhill

From the porch of the gray stone Church of St. Mary in Credenhill, a village not far from Hereford, Traherne, now the rector, could have looked out over a striking landscape as he developed his poem.

> *The Sun, that gilded all the bordering Woods,*
> > *Shone from the Sky*
> > *To beautify*
> *My Earthly and my Heavenly Goods;*
> > *Exalted in his Throne on high,*
> > *He shed his Beams*
> > *In golden Streams*
> *That did illustrat all the Sky;*
> *Those Floods of Light which he displays,*
> > *Did fill the glittr'ing Ways,*
> *While that unsufferable piercing Ey*
> > *The Ground did glorify.* [6]

Credenhill was a time of joyous, but disciplined concentration for Traherne on the quest for felicity and for communion with God through an enlargement of his capacities to love God and all the creation. "When I came into the Country, and being seated among silent Trees, had all my Time in mine own Hands, I resolved to Spend it all, whatever it cost me, in Search of Happiness, and to Satiat that burning Thirst which Nature had Enkindled, in me from my Youth. In which I was so resolut, that I chose rather to liv upon 10 pounds a yeer, and to go in Lether Clothes, and feed upon Bread and Water, so that I might hav all my time clearly to my self . . . " (III,46).

At Credenhill he came to know Susanna Hopton for whom he would later write the *Centuries of Meditations*. Mrs. Hopton lived about fifteen miles from Credenhill at Kington, where she had in her house an extended religious family of which Traherne was a member. It was much like the community of Nicolas Ferrar at Little Gidding. A militant Episcopalian and a royalist, Mrs. Hopton had showed her defiance of the Puritan Commonwealth by becoming a Roman Catholic, only to return to the Church of England upon the Restoration. For his services to the crown her affluent husband Richard received land and leases in Herefordshire and also a chief justiceship on the Welsh circuit. Traherne's brother Philip married Mrs. Hopton's only neice. Traherne had a reputation for talking with any one whom he might meet about the principles of felicity, often much to the embarrassment or impatience of the person confronted. In his lack of self-consciousness and his directness, Traherne shows many of the qualities of St. Francis. He "thought that he was to treat every man in the Person of Christ. That is both as if Himself were Christ in the Greatness of his Lov, and also as if the Man were Christ . . . for he was well acquainted with this Mystery, That evry man being the Object of our Saviors Lov, was to be treated as our Savior. Who hath said, 'Inasmuch as ye hav done it to the least of these my Brethren, ye hav done it unto me' " (IV, 28).

To London

In 1667, perhaps through the influence of the Hoptons, Traherne became private chaplain to Sir Orlando Bridgman, Lord Keeper of the Seal and previously president at the trial of the regicides. Traherne lived in Bridgman's London town house and in his villa at Teddington where he ministered part-time in the parish church. Freed from regular parish duties, Traherne spent five

years in intense literary production writing *Roman Forgeries,
Christian Ethicks,* and the private meditations for Susanna
Hopton, separated now from her by "a hundred miles." "I hav
had all things plentifully provided for me, without any Care at all,
my very Study of Felicity making me more to Prosper, then all the
Care in the Whole World" (III,46). In November 1672 Sir
Orlando was rudely deprived of his office by the King.
Humiliated, he retired at once to Teddington, dying within two
years. Traherne boldly dedicated his *Roman Forgeries* in 1673
to Sir Orlando and stayed on with the family until his own death in
October 1674. He was buried appropriately under the reading
desk of the church in Teddington. He had been unable to proof-
read *Christian Ethicks* which he had gotten to the printers. He
willed his hat and his books to his brother Philip who had been ordained and became an excellent scholar in Greek and Arabic,
serving as Anglican chaplain at Smyrna. Philip had also become
something of a snob, changing the family name to Traheron and
securing a coat of arms. He unfortunately began to "correct" his
brother's poetry and prose, creating a disaster. Confusion about
what was written by Thomas and what corrected by Philip has
probably held back a just evaluation of Thomas' poetry.

Writings

Roman Forgeries is not just another book of polemic in the long
series on conflicting doctrines stemming from the English Reformation. It is a careful historical analysis of sources in the spirit of
the new scientific movement of the seventeenth century that was
permeating all areas of human thought. It demonstrates the
analytical mind of a prosecutor doing for the early councils of the
church just that critical analysis and exposure of forged insertions
which Dr. James had asked for in his earlier *Corruption of the
Fathers* (1611). Another section of Traherne's book refutes the
False Decretals and the so-called Donation of Constantine. What
is especially interesting to us is Traherne's genuine amazement
that anyone could conceive of religious truth as being in contra-
diction to historical truth. Traherne here belongs to that liberal
movement within Anglicanism that would emphasize the role of
reason as an authority for enhancing the credibility of belief.

Unpublished Prose Works of Traherne

Other writings of Thomas Traherne have come to us through devious routes such as incorrect attribution to Mrs. Hopton or simply anonymously. Dr. George Hickes, a friend of Mrs. Hopton, published in 1699 *A Serious and Pathetical Contemplation of the Mercies of God in several most Devout and Sublime Thanksgivings for the Same.* Any reader of Traherne can recognize them at once as by him in their special diction, their waves of poetical prose, the rhythm of the Psalms and the cadences of the *Book of Common Prayer.* Some are so intimate that they were obviously not intended for publication. They provide, however, interesting autobiographical details: he gives thanks for his "household stuff—books, utensils, furniture" or for his sociable nature in having been made "a lover of company." There is a moving Prayer for the Nation that show his passionate Englishness. One thanksgiving especially leads us to see his sense of divine vocation in imitation of Christ. The lines wash back and forth like waves with an incoming tide.

> *O my Lord, make me like thee!*
> *A Son of God,*
> *In my love to Sinners . . .*
> *Let my love be Genuine, Divine, and Free.*
> *And for the delight I take,*
> *To rescue and to save them,*
> *To exalt and crown them,*
> *Let me pour out my self,*
> *My Spirit, Soul and Blood,*
> *My Time, Labour, Health, Estate, Life and all.*
> *O'tis Heavenly, Divine, Angelical!*
> *The glorious Victory over all the world*
> *Is love continuing beyond unkindness;*
> *Fill my love with Zeal of thine*
> *Like thine, O Lord, I desire it should be;*
> *A flame of thirsting Industry,*
> *Outliving hatred . . .*
> *Forgive my former {* *Flatness / Intermission / Deadness:*

> *Let me love every Person as Jesus Christ:*
> *Meet his love, and thine, O Lord,*
> *In every person . . .*
> *O Learn me this, and the whole is learned.*
> *Learn me this, the Divine Art,*
> *And the Life of God!*[7]

The *Hexameron*, meditations on the six days of creation, was published in 1717. Also in the same year Spinckes published *Meditations and Devotions on the Life of Christ* as Mrs. Hopton's own because the manuscript to which he had access was in her handwriting. What he had, however, was the original form of a work by Traherne written expressly for Mrs. Hopton and copied by her. Part of this work had already been published by Philip Traherne in 1685 as *The Soul's Communion with her Saviour*, the book which supplied Dobell with the clue to the identity of Thomas Traherne. These meditations on incidents in Christ's life adapted to the reader's condition contain much more about sinfulness and discipline than are to be found in Traherne's later *Centuries of Meditations* even taking into consideration the meditations on the cross in the first century. There are comments such as this one on the arrest of Jesus in the garden of Gethsemane: "Who, O Lord, could have bound thine omnipotent Hands, if Love had not bound them first?" The meditations help us to see that the stages and development of Traherne's mysticism tended to reflect the common pattern of Western mysticism: (1) the awakening of the soul to God, (2) the purgation of the soul, (3) its illumination, or the contemplative state as such, (4) the dark night of the soul bringing with it an even more severe purgation and finally (5) the union of the self with God. We also possess a notebook with liturgical meditations appropriate for the chief days of the church's year from Easter to All Saints' Day which Traherne probably intended for publication. The section from Advent to Good Friday has been lost from what Margoliouth has decided to call *The Church's Year-Book*. This document is extremely important for it shows the degree to which Traherne's devotion has been shaped by the *Book of Common Prayer* and how he in turn sought to mold the meditative life of others by its structures and sacred disciplines of time and space. For Traherne the individual and personal appeared to flow from the corporate experience of God in public worship. *The Church's Year-Book* has been influenced by Andrewes, Donne and Herbert and by Sparrow's *Rationale Upon the Book of Common Prayer.* In 1964 the discovery of a new manuscript, *Select Meditations,* was revealed by James Osborn, but it has not yet been edited or published. Also arranged in centuries, it apparently reflects at times some of the earlier stages of the material in *Centuries of Meditations,* but refers more directly to the mystical experience that underlies Traherne's classic.

Christian Ethicks

In 1675, a few months after Traherne's death, *Christian Ethicks* appeared with the ascription: "By Thomas Traherne, B.D., author of *The Roman Forgeries.*" It is somewhat conventional in form, closely following Aquinas and Aristotle, but actually very Platonic in content without becoming dualistic or depreciating the body. It refers with approval to *The Whole Duty of Man* published just before the Restoration and attacks the materialism of Thomas Hobbes' *Leviathan.* If the *Centuries of Meditations* shows his private communion with a friend, with himself, and with God the *Christian Ethicks* exhibits him as the reasoned theologian at home in the world of books and intent on melding a philosophical view of reality with the mystical quest for union with God. He tells us that he will not spend time analyzing the types and ways of sin and alienation, but that he will concentrate upon whatever is true, good and beautiful. The virtues for which gratitude is the incentive belong to all three periods in God's dispensation, the lost period of innocence, the present period of trial and grace, and the final period of glory even now breaking into our earthly lives. Virtues like repentance and patience which Traherne calls "the harsh and sour virtues," while absolutely indispensable for the period of trial and grace, are by their limitation to only one of the periods less suitable in Traherne's view for the grounding of a truly Christian ethic than the more basic wisdom, love and righteousness, to use one of his triadic lists. As in the *Centuries of Meditations,* the emphasis is upon the beauty of holiness. We are left feeling that his intellectual work is simply the transposition of worship into a new key. It is difficult for us to conceive of the intensity of Traherne's dedication to felicity. For him happiness is not the effect of chance or the by-product of some other commitment as it is generally regarded today. Happiness, rather, is the direct ethical

result of a wise and good life and the deliberately-sought fruition
of the soul's destined union with God. Perhaps the closest
analogy we have today to this kind of dedication is the ideal of the
scientist pledged to the pursuit of truth.

Christian Ethicks is not at all concerned with cases of conscience; it is a sustained argument for mysticism as the rational
way of life. Much is owed to the Renaissance Platonists and to
Hermes Trismegistus. There are in the *Christian Ethicks* about
four pages of quotations from the *Poemander* by Hermes whom
Traherne in company with his contemporaries believed to be of
great antiquity. "Wherfore we must be bold to say, that an Earthly
Man is a Mortal God, and the Heavenly God is an Immortal
Man." This paradoxical saying from Hermes really expresses in a
dramatic way Traherne's belief in the God-like quality of the
human being because of his creation in the divine image and in
"the humanity of God" that expresses the inmost being of the God
who becomes incarnate for the sake of humankind. Where
Traherne breaks with Neoplatonism is in its view that evil arises
from necessity. Traherne has a more biblical perspective.
Reference to the first of Henry More's Divine Dialogues is further
evidence for understanding Traherne as a member of the movement represented by the Cambridge Platonists. The recovery of
vision rather than redemption from sin is the motivating force
behind Traherne's ethics. His book was the only systematic study
of ethics in English intended for the educated laity to appear for a
period of about thirty years after the Restoration. It is a defense of
the joys of the senses as the royal road to felicity, a type of
"Christian epicureanism" as Traherne facetiously called it. The
rhythms of his prose are often like poetry and his images have
poetic quality. There are the images of water, the oceans, the
streams, springs and fountains. There are the Neoplatonic pictures
of light, the sun, the moon, the stars and the everyday objects of
existence bathed in a sparkling radiance. Mirrors, abysses and the
antipodes are frequently mentioned to further the paradox that by
looking down into a reflecting pool we actually see above. The
antitheses are short and sharp: "things Strange yet Common;
Incredible, yet Known; Most High, yet Plain; infinitely Profitable,
but not Esteemed" (I,3).

Poetry

Traherne's poetry can at times have great power and imaginative images, though he often seems incapable of maintaining the song through many stanzas. His poetry is therefore best read in small crystals rescued from their matrix. Gladys Wade suggests that he may have felt it his duty to write poetry because he so much admired David, then considered to be the poet of the Psalter. His work, however, is free from the metaphysical conceits that afflict some of his older contemporaries of the seventeenth century. Milton and Traherne for both of whom paradise was a basic theme died in 1674 at the ages of 66 and 37 respectively. Traherne's subjects are basically three and in this order: (1) childhood as a parable of the Kingdom of God; (2) Man as intermediary between God and the rest of creation; and (3) the wonder of the human mind. The first stanza "On Christmas-Day" is an illustration of Traherne's use of the heroic couplet and the stanza of varying complexity—both forms reflecting the poetic fashions of his day.

> Shall Dumpish Melancholy spoil my Joys
> While Angels sing
> And Mortals ring
> My Lord and Savior's Prais!
> Awake from Sloth, for that alone destroys,
> 'Tis Sin defiles, 'tis Sloth puts out thy Joys.
> See how they run from place to place,
> And seek for Ornaments of Grace;
> Their Houses deckt with sprightly Green,
> In Winter makes a Summer seen;
> They Bays and Holly bring
> As if 'twere Spring![8]

There are ten stanzas repeating this four rhyme scheme as abbaaaccddbb with the rhyme b (sing, ring, bring, spring) identical throughout, suggesting very effectively the continuous chiming of the Christmas bells. Some of his finest poems are "The Salutation," "Wonder," "The Approach," "The Circulation," "Desire," "Goodness," and "On News." (The last is well known because of its inclusion in the Oxford Book of English Verse.)

The Centuries of Meditations

The Centuries of Meditations, judging by internal evidence,

belong chiefly to that five year period of intense literary activity in London and Teddington as Sir Orlando's chaplain. Traherne wrote his two published books, *Roman Forgeries* and *Christian Ethicks*, worked on the poetry, and produced the *Church's Year Book* and *Meditations and Devotions on the Life of Christ*.

The *Centuries*, a kind of *Pilgrim's Progress* of the once-born soul, are without precedent in literature although they show the influence of Augustine and his followers. They well up from the depths of Traherne's experience, but have also been worked over, much as a stream rounds a pebble. Each meditation has its own integrity, but it also offers material for future meditations and recollects past meditations. There is a definite scheme of presentation and development although there are numerous digressions and eddy currents. They are sustained by Traherne's practice of meditation and by his perspective that all activity is really the continuation of worship. Because there is so much autobiography and exposition of the principles on felicity for Susanna Hopton " . . . at 100 miles distance," with the crossing out of some of the more intimate references some commentators have failed to understand the continuous reality of the mystical piety that undergirds the *Centuries*: "If you will be lazy, and not Meditat, you lose all" (IV,95). "To be Acquainted with celestial Things is not only to know them, but by frequent Meditation to be familiar with them" (IV, 96).

One of the charming qualities of the *Centuries* is pithy expression and often ironic humor. "For there is Great Difference between a Worm and a Cherubim" (I,38). "A little Grit in the Ey destroyeth the sight of the very Heavens: and a little Malice or Envy a World of Joys" (IV,17). "Awaken thy Soul, be an Enlarged Seraphim" (II,51). "The Ocean bounded in a finit Shore, Is better far becaus it is no more" (III,21). "A Sight of Happiness is Happiness" (III,60). "A Christian is an Oak flourishing in Winter" (IV,91).

"The First Century" begins with an acknowledgment of his friend Susanna Hopton and of his purpose to communicate to her vital truths. "I hav a Mind to fill this (book) with Profitable Wonders. And since Love made you put it into my Hands I will fill it with those Truths you Love, without knowing them . . . " (I,1) Traherne is not at all diffident about his mission. "I will open my Mouth in Parables: I will utter Things that have been Kept Secret from the foundation of the World" (I,3). Holding that contemplation of eternity makes the soul immortal, he can "visit Noah in His Ark and swim upon the Waters of the Deluge"(I,55).

Already in the "First Centurie" we are introduced to created objects as a ladder leading us to God. But this theological commonplace is lifted from the page of a book to become an exciting personal journey of discovery in what must surely be called an "ecological mysticism." It is his special gift to us today. Traherne has a sense of Loren Eisley's mystical identification and participation in nonhuman forms of life. This mystical identification is based on the principle of the relatedness of all things. Pierre Teilhard de Chardin also writes of our being the thousandth cousin to an amoeba and of our relationship to seaweed. "You never Enjoy the world aright," writes Traherne, "till the Sea it self floweth in your Veins, till you are Clothed with the Heavens, and Crowned with the Stars" (I,29). Love is the bond of union between all creatures. "By Lov our souls are married and sodderd to the creatures" (II,66). It is an organic understanding of the human relationship to the whole cosmos made possible by Traherne's feeling that through being created in the image of God a person becomes a co-creator with God himself, " . . . for herby I perceived that we were to liv the Life of God: when we lived the tru life of Nature according to Knowledg" (III,58). "His attitude toward nature," comments Gladys Wade, "is something new in our literature; and this is the secret of that strange effect of beauty. The part, every tiniest fragment of it, is for him flooded by the light of the whole . . . "[9] He understands that the ecological relatedness of the creation is not only grace, but can also be turned into judgment, a perception being driven home to us today by pollution, the eradication of flora and fauna, and the diminished quality of life. "Yea one Act only of Despite done to the smallest Creature made you infinitely deformed" (II,30). In his poem "Dumnesse" the creation is seen as mediator between God and humankind.

> The Heavens were an Orakle, and spake
> Divinity: The Earth did undertake
> The office of a Priest . . . [10]

To desire felicity, however, is not the same thing as having it. Traherne believes it can be won only by intense discipline and the meditational path of communing with all things until a perception of their glory and beauty and a lively sense of their interrelationships yields a conviction of their spiritual reality. The ontology becomes Platonic without the dualism of Platonism. The spiritual power of the human imagination can create worlds even more beautiful than our universe. We see here the divine dimension of humanity. "The World within you is an offering returned. Which is infinitely more Acceptable to GOD Almighty, since it came from him, that it might return unto Him. Wherein the Mysterie is Great. For GOD hath made you able to Creat Worlds in your own mind, which are more Precious unto Him then those which He Created . . ." (II,90).

The perception of the beauty of the universe is the ladder of perfection whereby we climb to God not to escape this life but to see this life savingly transfigured in everyday things. In the latter part of the "First Centurie" there are meditations upon the cross that suggest his other *Meditations on the Life of Christ*. They establish beyond any doubt the Christological orientation of Traherne's thought and the centrality for him, despite his unwillingness to wallow in expressions of sinfulness, of the Incarnation and Atonement of Christ. Although Traherne's concepts of the Cross are largely Anselmian his piety about it is patristic in quality. His principle of the coinherence of all reality finds its climax as the Son, through whom all things were made, dies upon the sacred tree to which all of creation silently bows in adoration. "To this poor Bleeding Naked Man did all the Corn and Wine and Oyl, and Gold and Silver in the World minister in an invisible Maner, even as he was exposed Lying and Dying upon the Cross" (I,60). Traherne's devotion to the cross reshapes the old image of the tree by a fresh insight into invisible flame. "That Cross is a Tree set on fire with invisible flame, that Illuminateth all the World. The Flame is Lov" (I,60). Prayers are addressed to "Jesu" as Traherne uses the old vocative case: "fill me with thy Holy Spirit, and make my Soul and Life Beautifull" (I,96).

"The Second Centurie"

The "Second Centurie" like the movement of a symphony repeats the motiv of the world serving the needs of humanity. It passes beyond the meditations on the Cross in the previous century to a reflection on how much we stand in need of the Atonement. Traherne's complete break with the unmoved mover of his

background in Greek philosophy is nowhere clearer. Traherne's
God acts and suffers as he identifies himself with the plight of his
creatures. Like Frederick Maurice, Traherne reads the principle of
sacrifice on Calvary back into the eternal relationships of the Son
to the Father. "It is as if from all Eternity He had suffered for us"
(II,37). Love is described in the Trinitarian terms of Augustine and
is seen as the force behind human activity. "You are as Prone to
lov, as the Sun is to shine" (II,65). If God is act, then the soul is
act. Traherne describes its greatness. Philosophers have all fallen
short in their attempts to describe and define happiness. "God,"
says Traherne in an adaptation of the insight of the mystics, "is . . .
more near to us then we are to our selvs. So that we cannot feel
our Souls, but we must feel Him" (II,81).

"The Second Centurie" ends on a note of exaltation and
suggests the further themes that will be developed. "So that who-
soever will Profit in the Mystry of Felicity, must see the Objects of
His Happiness, and the Maner how they are to be Enjoyed, and
discern also the Powers of His Soul by which He is to enjoy them,
and perhaps the Rules that shall Guid Him in the Way of Enjoyment. All which you have here GOD, THE WORLD, YOUR
SELF. All Things in Time and Eternity being the Objects of your
felicity GOD the Giver, and you the Receiver" (II,100).

"The Third Centurie"

"The Third Centurie" is probably the best known because of the
charming way in which Traherne communicates autobiographical
details, especially of his childhood. Numerous quotations have
already been used from it in the section of this essay on his life.
"Certainly Adam in Paradice had not more sweet and Curious
Apprehensions of the World, then I when I was a child" (III,1).
There is a quality in Traherne's evaluation of childlikeness
comparable to Blake's in his Songs of Innocence; it is apparent in
Traherne's poems "The Salutation," "Wonder," "Eden" and
"Innocence." Traherne in obedience to the gospel injunction has
set "the little child in the midst," knowing with Wordsworth that
heaven lay about him in his infancy. "All apeared New, and
Strange at the first, inexpressibly rare, and Delightfull, and
Beautifull. I was a little Stranger which at my Enterance into the
World was Saluted and Surrounded with innumerable Joys. My
Knowledg was Divine. I knew by Intuition those things which

since my Apostasie, I Collected again, by the Highest Reason"
(III,2). What Traherne is saying to us is that we must be born
again, that childhood happiness has been deliberately implanted
in our soul as a foretaste of mature felicity through the pressure of
continuing memory.

Traherne's doubts in a time just before or just after going to the
university, which have been described earlier, are given a vivid
expression at one time of great and atypical discomfort. "Another
time, in a Lowering and sad Evening, being alone in the field,
when all things were dead and quiet, a certain Want and Horror
fell upon me, beyond imagination. The unprofitableness and
Silence of the Place dissatisfied me, its Wideness terrified me,
from the utmost Ends of the Earth fears surrounded me" (III,23).
Traherne describes the stages by which the Bible acquired for him
the character of a credible revelation. After the university came
the move into the country parish at Credenhill with its total con-
secration to and concentration upon the principles of felicity.
Traherne's prose shows the poetical rhythms of the Psalms. Re-
iteration in the Psalms became so much a part of his style that the
elimination of the second synonym comprised his most common
correction in his own revision of the *Centuries*. The Psalms with
their approach to God through the beauty of holiness and the
ladder of the creatures made the Bible at last authentic for
Traherne. " . . . the Way of Communion with God in all Saints, as
I saw Clearly in the Person of David. Me thoughts a New Light
Darted in into all his Psalmes, and finaly spread abroad over the
whole Bible . . . GOD by this means bringing me into the very
Heart of His Kingdom" (III,66). Traherne paid his tribute to David
in a poem of eight stanzas, only the first of which is quoted.

> *In Salem dwelt a Glorious King,*
> *Raisd from a Shepherds lowly State,*
> *That did his Praises like an Angel sing*
> *Who did the World create.*
> *By many great and Bloody Wars,*
> *He was Advanced unto Thrones:*
> *But more Delighted in the Stars,*
> *Then in the Splendor of His Precious Stones.*
> *Nor Gold nor Silver did his Ey regard:*
> *The Works of GOD were his Sublime Reward.* (III,69, stanza 1)

It could be said that four biblical texts are the foundation blocks for
Traherne's temple building: (1) "God is love;" (2) "God so loved
the world;" (3) "You are sons of God;" (4) "that we may be filled
with all the fullness of God."

The Fourth and Fifth "Centuries"

The "Fourth Centurie" shifts from the "I" form of narration to
the third person, but the use becomes inconsistent when in especially strong moments of emotion Traherne reverts to personal
narration. Perhaps out of modesty he sought to reduce the seeming self-righteousness of the claim that he practiced the principles
of felicity or perhaps he began to think of publishing the *Centuries*
at some future time and thought the more impersonal third person
more appropriate. Traherne's high evaluation of philosophy, the
form and intensity of which clearly places him among the Cambridge Platonists who were at that time getting under way as a
movement, is reflected in a familiar sentence from him. "He
thought that to be a Philosopher, A Christian and a Divine was to
be one of the most Illustrious Creatures in the World . . . for either
of these Three include the other two" (IV,3). Twenty-four
principles of felicity are then discussed. Fifteen meditations relate
self-love to love of others as an enabling step along the way. The
saintly quality of Traherne shines through his own accomplish-
ment in this area. "It is more Glorious to lov others, and more desirable, but by Natural Means to be attained. That Pool must first
be filled, that shall be made to overflow. He was ten yeers studying before he could satisfy his Self Lov. And now finds nothing
more easy then to lov others better than oneself. And that to love
Mankind so is the comprehensiv Method to all felicity" (IV,55).
Sacrificial love which Traherne believed characterized the life of
God from all eternity is seen as empowering sacrificial love in
people. This human love, Traherne believes, is momentous for
world history. His warning to us is *love or perish*. "It is seldom
considered; but a Lov to others Stronger then what we bear to
ourselvs, is the Mother of all the Heroick Actions that hav made
Histories pleasant and Beautified the World" (IV,60). Gladys
Wade, commenting on Traherne's view of love as the universal
quality of harmonious being, writes: "we shall not find in all
literature the sublime beauty of 'naked and divested Love' in its
true perfection sung with greater wisdom or more moving

power"[11]. Traherne is no quietist. Christian love must issue in action or else it is not Christian love. There is something completely practical and everyday about him. "The Soul is made for Action, and cannot rest, till it be employd. Idlenes is its Rust . . . If therefore you would be Happy, your Life must be as full of Operation, as God of Treasure" (IV,95).

The "Fifth Centurie" consists of only ten entries, giving rise to the speculation that they remain unfinished due to his final illness in September 1674. Margoliouth, the editor of the critical edition of Traherne, however, argues that the content and themes have reached their appropriate conclusion as it is. What we have discovered in Traherne is a sort of double helix in which the journey outward is related to the journey inward with repetition of its treatment at each stage of advance in terms of the threefold human estate of innocence, fall and redemptive recovery of vision. If this pattern is really the shape of the *Centuries*, then the "Fifth Centurie" needed a fuller treatment of love of God than Traherne in his failing health was able to supply. He also wrote the Number "11" with no entry after it in the manuscript.

Traherne, however, summarizes in the final sentence his themes of the infinity of time and space under the infinity of God for the illimitable soul of humankind. Here is a crescendo of confidence and exultation and happiness: "The Essence of God therefore being all Light and Knowledg, Lov and Goodness, Care and Providence, felicity and Glory, a Pure and simple Act; it is present in its Operations, and by those Acts which it eternaly exerteth, is wholly Busied in all Parts and places of his Dominion, perfecting and compleating our Bliss and Happiness" (IV,10).

In Traherne we find an amazing union of the intuitive and the intellectual, the aesthetical and the ethical, and the practical and the devotional with which almost nothing in the history of mysticism can really be compared. It could be said of him that he expressed the comprehensiveness of Anglicanism in his spirituality.

Footnotes

[1] Whenever the *Centuries of Meditations* are quoted their location will be indicated by means of a Roman numeral for the number of the *Centurie* (there are five) and an Arabic number for the paragraph in parentheses in the text immediately following the quotation. The text is taken from H. M. Margoliouth, *Thomas Traherne: Centuries, Poems, and Thanksgivings* (Oxford: Clarendon Press, 1958) 2 Vols. This is the critical edition.

[2] Gladys I. Wade, *Thomas Traherne* (Princeton: Princeton University Press, 1946), p. 210.

[3] Bertram Dobell, *Centuries of Meditations* (London: P. J. and A. E. Dobell, 1927), pp. viii, xii-xiii.

[4] John Masefield, *The Speaker*, April 1903.

[5] Anthony à Wood, *Athenae Oxonienses* (ed. Bliss, 1813-20).

[6] "The World" from H. M. Margoliouth *op. cit.* vol. II p. 94.

[7] Ibid. II, pp. 267-8.

[8] Ibid. II, p. 110.

[9] G. I. Wade, *op. cit.* p. 234.

[10] H. M. Margoliouth, *op. cit.* II, p.44

[11] G. I. Wade, *op. cit.* pp. 187-8.

V

Christian Spirituality: From Wilberforce to Temple

John E. Booty

Introduction: *William Temple and "Other Worldliness"*

On June 10, 1918, William Temple preached a sermon at Repton School on Colossians 3:1-3, a passage that expresses both the meaning of Christian spirituality and the problem it poses for moderns. Here is Temple's text:

> "If then ye were raised together with Christ, seek the things that are above, where Christ is, seated on the right hand of God. Set your mind on things that are above, not on things that are upon the earth. For ye died, and your life is hid with Christ in God."

Christian spirituality concerns living in Christ, fellowship with God and openness to the work of the Holy Spirit whereby such living and fellowship occur and grow in scope and intensity. The first implication is that spirituality thus described necessitates a renunciation of earthly things in order that the Christian may rise to new life in Christ. Understood in this way the text is virtually manichaean in its separation of the two spheres of human experience, the world and the spirit.

Temple, who calls his sermon "Other Worldliness," provides another interpretation. With Christian Socialism, the social Gospel, and other similar developments in mind, the clergyman who will become the Archbishop of Canterbury, claims that a change has been in progress "as profound as that of the Reformation itself."[1] That change has been from concern for salvation in another world to concern for life in the world where we presently live. The older view tended toward self-centeredness and the perpetuation of human pain and social injustice. Temple allowed that the view of the Christian life and salvation held by his ancestors essentially concerned this world as well as the other, but he claimed that the tendency was revealed when William Wilberforce, the Evangelical parliamentarian at the beginning of the nineteenth century, solaced the poor by pointing to the shortness of life and the greatness of the rewards awaiting them in heaven. The tendency was also revealed by a speaker at the General Assembly of the Church of Scotland who claimed that Christians should have no concern at all for this passing world. Temple then said:

> "Over against that old view is the conviction that we are called as Christians to the service of God here and now; that on earth as in heaven His Name is to be hallowed, His Kingdom to come, and His Will to be done. For that Christ taught us to pray; for that He has summoned us to work. Not there but here is the sphere of our spiritual concern; not then but now is salvation to be won and made manifest. The Christian's duty in regard to slums is not merely to tell the inhabitants that their squalor is of small consequence because soon they will pass to the house of many mansions. The Christian duty in regard to sweated-labour is not merely to comfort the oppressed with the reminder that earthly conditions are transient, but to destroy the system which makes such sweating possible."[2]

Temple is not, however, here advocating a total immersion in the earthly present. So to immerse oneself is to be implicated in two weaknesses against which the older view stood guard: one is "moral solvenliness," the view that everyday duties are too small to concern us, the other is that materialism which elevates things above people, physical conditions above "the characters of men and women." The point is that "if we are to be in earnest with the new religious outlook which has been given in our time, it means that we are to live in this world by the principles and in the power of the other world."[3] As animals we are properly concerned with the physical but if we stay at the animal level of existence we shall be denying an essential part of our true nature, that spiritual capacity which transcends the physical and orders it. "Progress is the increasing control of the spiritual over the animal in man." Temple suggests that living at this "higher" level—being true to our nature as created in the image of God—means "a new devotion to the entirely dull duties of every day," keeping "alive by prayer and communion your intercourse with God," and realizing "your membership in the Church."[4] Practically speaking, as World War I is ending, this spiritual orientation involves a choice concerning "foundation-principles":

"Are we going to build again upon competing selfishness and mutual distrust? Or are we going to try this time to build on the one truth of all things, the revealed nature of God, the supremacy of Love? Are we, in other words, going at last to recognise that all forms of self-seeking, in man or in nation, are really self-destructive? 'He that would save his life, the same shall lose it.' Only in service of what lies beyond ourselves, only in service of the Kingdom of God . . . is peace or joy to be found."

With that the right understanding of the text from Colossians can be stated:

"We are to live here as citizens of the Kingdom of God. And we can only do that truly and effectively if our affections are set on things above, that is to say, on love and beauty and truth, whose value is in themselves and cannot be touched by accident or by death; not on things on the earth—greatness or honour or riches or any other thing whose value is determined by comparison between our selves and other people."[5]

Then, in a passage reminiscent of Jewel, Hooker, Andrewes, Hall, Donne and Herbert when they focus attention on the sacrifice of Christ on the Cross, Temple directs our attention to Christ:

"Think of Him then, the Hero-Redeemer, 'Who for the joy that was set before Him,' the joy of a world won by Him for His Father's Kingdom, 'endured the Cross in scorn of contempt'; hear Him as He pleads with your self-will, obey Him as He calls to sacrifice. In Him, and nowhere else, is the power by which you must serve Him. 'Ye died': in comparison with the claim that is made, you found yourself helpless; 'your life hath been hid with Christ in God.' There, if you will but seek and find it, is the power that can once more 'turn the world upside down.' "[6]

Temple's sermon illumines Christian spirituality as the totality of life lived not for self, either for the self's comfort and enjoyment or the self's salvation, but as life lived in Christ for the sake of the world in our time, that love may prevail over all that is contrary. Through living such a life we grow in grace, which is to say that we grow in humanity, becoming daily more fully that which we are meant to be, servants of the living God and of God's world, striving for peace and for justice, struggling against all of those powers and principalities, all demonic machines and blood-thirsty

tyrannies that threaten our spiritual as much as our physical
survival. Christian spirituality involves growing into the fulness of
the stature of Christ, the Incarnate Son of God in whom there is
revealed the law of the universe and the law of our being,
sacrificial love.

The separation of this world from another is misleading. It is as
though there were "two worlds." Seeking that which is above
implies a Ptolemaic view of the universe contrary to the universe
as we know it. And yet the truth of Colossians 3:1-3 is apparent.
Whatever metaphysical terms we may use, experience teaches us
that we are creatures who, left to our own devices, are animals,
vulnerable to influences within and without that would destroy us.
Christian spirituality involves our acknowledging and claiming our
transcendence in relation to the transcendent Reality from which
our uniqueness is derived, that Reality from which we come, and
toward which we are moving. Human self-transcendence, when
not subdued by that materialism defined as the physical governing
us and destroying our ability to perceive and pursue beauty,
goodness and truth, is a mirror of the divine, the ultimate Reality
as seen and known in Jesus Christ. To achieve that which is most
definitively human is to arrive at a state of grace and find oneself
at the point of intersection between creation and fulfillment, time
and eternity, where we enter into communion with God through
the action of the divine Spirit and grow into a fuller and fuller
realization of humanity.

Christian spirituality properly focuses attention upon the illusive
Holy Spirit. John V. Taylor speaks of the "Ground of our
meeting" (as distinguished from the "Ground of our being") and
of the Holy Spirit "as the elemental energy of communion itself,
within which all separate existences may be made present and
personal to each other." Later he speaks of the Holy Spirit as "the
familiar third party who stands between me and the other making
us mutually aware." The Holy Spirit draws us out of our self preoccupation into self-transcendence, opening our eyes to others
in Christ, "or the point of need, or the heart-breaking brutality and
the equally heart-breaking beauty of the world." Thus the Holy
Spirit "is the giver of that vision without which the people perish."[7]
Christian spirituality involves the operating of the Holy Spirit to
enliven our human spirits. It also involves what Gabriel Marcel has
called "availability," which is to say, openness to the Other and to
others in the Other, welcoming and receiving the Holy Spirit and

other spirits as the Holy Spirit brings us to meet with them. We have not yet mentioned prayer, but now is the moment to do so, recalling that Marcel described availability best when defining the spirit of prayer: "The spirit of prayer, above all, is a welcoming (*accueillante*) disposition towards everything which can tear me away from myself, from my propensity to become hypnotized by my own faults."[8] Christian spirituality thus involves liberation from servitude to the self, for service to God (*litourgia*) and to the world God loves (*diakonia*). Such a view is not totally foreign to Anglican tradition. It brings to mind Thomas Cranmer's understanding of communion and Holy Communion; Richard Hooker's key concept of participation (*koinonia; menō, menein*); and Lancelot Andrewes' rich and penetrating understanding of Christ's sacrifice represented through the Holy Mysteries eliciting the Christian's *tergemina hostea*, triple offering of the soul by prayer, the body by abstinence, and our goods by "alms-deeds."[9] Anglicanism tends to understand spirituality in terms of self-transcendent activity patterned after the revelation of the law of the universe as shown on the Cross, the law of sacrifice.

In that which follows some features of the development of Anglican spirituality in the nineteenth and twentieth century shall be presented. My presentation is not exhaustive but rather tends to follow the trail as begun in this introduction. Along the way we shall concentrate upon some, not all, who have some claim to have understood the tradition and to have been influential in perpetuating it. Not all of them will be recognizable as "experts" in whatever the field of Christian spirituality may be, but they have all influenced those of us in this particular communion and fellowship of the Church, either directly or indirectly through others.

The Spirituality of the English Evangelicals: Conformed to Christ

We begin with the point of transition to which Temple referred and in particular with the Evangelicals and the Anglo-Catholics (Tractarians and Ritualists). I put these two major movements together because where spirituality is concerned they share much. Both were engaged in the pursuit of holiness at a time when the English seemed to be increasingly preoccupied with the pursuit of self-gain, of things and of power at whatever cost to others. In this pursuit both movements developed a seriousness and an interiority which generated much of the power they so obviously possessed. Both struggled to relate the world of transcendent Deity to this world in order that the unseen might be seen, its power experienced and its commands obeyed. Both were concerned to transform this world by the power of the other world. They differed, of course, in the ways by which they sought to realize their goals and indeed collided violently along the way so that much of the power they conveyed into the world was dissipated in their opposition.

Anglican Evangelicalism stemmed from the evangelical revival of the eighteenth century. Grounded in the experience of conversion, evangelicals believed that the "corruption of our nature by the fall, and our recovery through Jesus Christ," were "the two leading truths of Christian religion." William Romaine (1714-1795) made that assertion and said that "a sinner will never seek after nor desire Christ farther than he feels his guilt and his misery; nor will he receive Christ by faith, till all other methods of saving himself fail; nor will he live upon Christ's fulness farther than he has an abiding sense of his own want of him."[10] The aim was conversion, acknowledged as the Lord's doing and yet requiring preparation and submission. Life after conversion involved an intensely active life of conformity to the standard of perfection made known in Jesus Christ. The faithful person "wishes to be like Christ, and to be more like him: he would feel more of the power of the Cross of Christ to crucify in him the body of sin, and more of the power of the risen Jesus, that there may be a real growth in him, and that in all things."[11]

The intensity of Evangelical spirituality was bred of such a desire for conformity to Christ and also of a fear of eternal damnation. This fear of being found wanting on Judgment Day resulted in intense prayer, self-examination and soul searching. Sarah Trimmer went into seclusion for two or three hours a week to examine her past conduct and to confer with her Maker about it. Henry Thornton, the pious banker, recorded the details of his self-examination in his diary, accusing himself, for instance, of staying too long in bed, not being conscientious enough in his study of the Bible, and lacking self denial in his inner thoughts and in his business dealings. William Wilberforce, the parliamentarian, wrote of the necessity of self denial, of renunciation of all that inhibited conformity to Christ, and of dedication of all that one is and all that one has to the service of God.[12] Such evangelicals have been accused of hypocrisy, of using their religion to keep down the lower classes and to enrich the rich, and of bringing into being a cult of manners contrary to the intent of the Gospel. Hannah More recognized the dangers involved in Evangelical piety and especially in the cultivation of a cult of manners. Thus the great woman leader of the movement wrote:

> "Christianity . . . is assuredly something more than a mere set of rules; and faith, though it never pretended to be the substitute for a useful life, is indispensably necessary to its acceptance with God. The Gospel never offers to make religion supercede morality, but everywhere clearly proves that morality is not the whole of religion."[13]

Hannah More points to "piety" as the prior obligation, "the best principle of moral conduct." Such piety involves intense prayer and self-examination in the light of the Cross and of Judgment Day. It also involves family prayers, all of the family, including servants and guests, being brought together daily, the head of the household presiding, the Bible being read, sometimes along with some portion of an edifying work such as Doddridge's *Family Expositor*, a psalm or hymn being sung, and then prayer, sometimes extempore, sometimes from some collection such as Henry Thornton's *Family Prayers* (1834).[14]

While some Evangelicals tended to slight public worship in the parish church in favor of personal and family devotions, most were "firmly attached to the Liturgy."[15] Charles Simeon (1759-1836) one of the most prominent Evangelical clerics, taught that "the scope and tendency of our Liturgy is to raise our minds to the holy and heavenly state, and to build us up upon the Lord Jesus Christ as the only foundation of a sinner's hope."[16] Simeon denounced those forms of worship dominated by party views and praised the excellency of the Prayer Book in which "truth, the whole truth, is brought forward without fear . . . but also without offence; all is temperate; all is candid; all is practical; all is peaceful, and every word is spoken in love."[17] Simeon did not regard the Prayer Book as perfect, but the greatest defect he located in the hearts of those who worship, resisting the power of the Liturgy. Thus he exhorted: "Let us bring with us into the presence of God that *spirituality of mind* that shall fit us for communion with Him, and that *purity of heart* which is the commencement of the Divine image in the soul."[18] The challenge to

Anglican Evangelical spirituality was to avoid the selfishness of an individualistic pursuit of personal salvation, that danger to which Temple pointed. So long as the Evangelicals maintained their piety within the context of corporate worship according to the *Book of Common Prayer* they were avoiding the chief dangers that confronted them and were, as Simeon indicated, involved in a Liturgy through which the Holy Spirit worked to bring them into communion with God.

Anglican Evangelicals were actively engaged in three areas of social action. First, they labored for the education of the poor. Their aim may have been to convert people but in the process they prepared many of the powerless in their society for the eventual exercise of power. Hannah More was no revolutionary. Fearful of the Jacobinism that ravaged the French monarchy, she sought to inculcate in her children the virtues of loyalty and obedience to superior powers. But by teaching the poor to read and to think she prepared them for protest and change. As Margaret Cropper has said, Hannah More "made a revolution in thought when in her tracts she 'let the poor know that the rich had faults.' "[19] The Evangelicals were instrumental in the abolition of the slave trade and of slavery in British possessions. Again they may have been more concerned for the conversion of people than for any radical change in society, but their piety led to a revolution effecting not only slavery but the sanctity of property. In addition, the campaign waged by William Wilberforce constituted a moral revolution arousing the consciences of people to regard all human beings as sacred and to labor for the weak and oppressed. Finally, the Evangelicals labored, again with mixed motives, to liberate women and children from enslavement to machines. The industrial revolution seized upon cheap, expendable labor. Women and children were grossly exploited. Lord Ashley, the Seventh Earl of Shaftesbury, led the battle for factory law reform. Again the impulse came from Evangelical piety. As Georgina Battiscombe has said, "The force that drove him [Shaftesbury] was a passionate concern for souls. He believed that factory children, chimney-sweeps, and lunatics all had souls to be saved and that very little time remained in which to save them."[20] Thanks to this concern for the salvation of souls, Hannah More and others labored against great odds but successfully for the education of the poor, Wilberforce and others succeeded in stopping the slave trade and slavery in British possessions, and

Lord Shaftesbury and others enacted legislation to protect human beings from the tyranny of machines and the gluttony of capitalists.

Evangelical spirituality was focused upon personal salvation, but in its insistence upon conformity to Christ it specified that such salvation involved such behavior as denounced sin and inhumanity and sought for the alleviation of ignorance, suffering and oppression. It was the piety that ultimately mattered, as Hannah More said, the fervent prayer and self-examination, personal and family devotions, and the public Liturgy of the church. The zeal for holiness prepared a way into the future when other worldliness would be renounced for this worldliness empowered from beyond.

Anglo-Catholicism and the Unseen Encroaching upon the Seen

The Oxford Movement of the period immediately following the Reform Act of 1832 was a part of a wider movement of protest against the government's interference in the affairs of the Church, especially considering that the government then contained members in no way belonging to the Church of England. That which distinguished the Oxford Movement from the wider movement of protest and from the High Churchmen of the Hackney Phalanx was a matter of spirituality or interiority, a zeal for holiness. As Basil Willey has said, the deepest concern of the Oxford Movement "was with the invisible world, not with politics or the obsolete; its driving power, a hunger and thirst after righteousness, an effort toward true sanctity."[21] Here we are strongly reminded of the beginnings of the evangelical revival in eighteenth century Oxford.

John Henry Newman had experienced a conversion as an Evangelical and it is clear that the Oxford Movement shared much with the Evangelicals, especially such fervent scholars as Romaine and Simeon. But they were also influenced by the Caroline Divines, and especially by Lancelot Andrewes and his *Preces Privatae*, those private devotions that Newman translated and had published. William Law and his *Serious Call to a Devout and Holy Life* influenced John Wesley and also various members of the Oxford Movement. All of these influences are observable in Newman's preaching. There in sermons delivered to spell-bound undergraduates and devout parishioners we find the heart of Tractarian spirituality. In a sermon on 2 Cor. 4:18, Newman stated that there is another world beyond the one we see, a world "more wonderful than the world we see, for this reason if for no other, that we do not see it." In the visible church we draw near to this other world. There we find a continuous coming and going between that world and this, so that as we pray, as we use the Name of Jesus or make the sign of the Cross, we employ power beyond any human power.

> "When we protest or confess or suffer in the Name of Christ, what are we but ourselves types and symbols of the Cross of Christ and of the strength of Him who died on it. When we are called to battle for the Lord, what are we who are seen, but mere outposts, the advanced guard of a mighty host, ourselves few in number and despicable, but bold beyond our numbers, because supported by chariots of fire and horses of fire round about the Mountain of the Lord of Hosts under which we stand?"[22]

The visible church depends upon the invisible world not upon any human powers. Indeed, the church is that portion of the invisible world that encroaches on the world we see. We can go further and say that the avenue by which the power of the invisible encroaches on the visible is provided in the sacraments administered by those standing in apostolic succession.

Expressed with passionate seriousness, this understanding of reality is powerful to form lives of moral rigor and fervent devotion. Edward Bouverie Pusey, the leader of the Movement after Newman's conversion to Rome, wrote and spoke forcefully of the Christian being dead to this world and alive to God. Baptism is the sacrament of death and life and the Christian's life is one of realizing that death in order that he or she may grow in newness of life, in righteousness, in holiness. What this means is indicated by Pusey when he says: "The less we live for things outward, the stronger burns our inward life. The more we live to things unseen, the less hold will this world of sense have over us."[23] In such other-worldliness we have the impetus for a renewal of Christian asceticism such as that of the Early Church, and for sacramental confession and the religious life such as blossomed in the medieval church and was evident in continental Roman Catholicism. In this piety there were also the grounds for the development of ritual and ceremonial expressive of the vision of the unseen encroaching upon the seen, in response to which

Christians are expected to renounce the seen to live daily more fully to things unseen.

Ritualism represents another stage in the development of Anglo-Catholicism. Newman and Pusey both had reservations concerning the ceremonial embellishment of the corporate worship, the decoration of church buildings, and the restoration of the vestments associated with the first *Book of Common Prayer* and the late medieval church. But the emphasis which men such as Newman and Pusey placed upon the church and on the Eucharist in particular as celebrated by clergy linked to the Apostles by succession, provided an aura of authority and mystery in which the unseen encroaches upon the seen and creates a strong urge toward ritualism. C. F. Lowder, the pugnacious ritualist priest, spoke of the ritual of St. Peter's, London Docks, as "the whole arrangement of the service typical of its heavenly counterpart." Influenced by Romanticism, but also by Hooker, Andrewes, and the rest of the Caroline Divines, ritualism, as Owen Chadwick has said, springs from "the desire to turn churches into houses of prayer and devotion, where men would let their hearts go outward in worship, instead of preaching houses where their minds would be argued into assent to creeds or to moral duties."[24]

The spirituality of the Oxford Movement, involving the encroachment of the unseen on the seen, was not without important social consequences. While it may be true, as W. G. Ward has stated, that "Tractarian intellect and spirituality converted awkwardly into policy,"[25] yet the intense personal asceticism, and the vision of the other world against this world, led to social action when the time was ripe. Newman bluntly said: "the Church was formed for the express purpose of interferring or (as irreligious men would say) meddling with the world."[26] Furthermore, there was a specific concern among the followers of Newman and Pusey for the urban poor. Pusey saw the face of Christ in the faces of the poor and knew that failure to serve them was failure to serve Him.[27] Through men such as Pusey the church was indeed becoming the conscience of the nation, seeking to transform it into the Kingdom of God by means of its sacramental ministry and the extension of that ministry in social service and, in time, social action. Ritualist priests such as Lowder, Stanton and Mackonochie plunged into the seething slums of London to serve the poor, evangelizing them and caring for their bodily and mental needs.

There was another strong impetus to Anglo-Catholicism's ministry in this world by the power of the other world. This came with an increased emphasis on the docrine of the Incarnation. Robert Isaac Wilberforce, the son of the Evangelical parliamentarian and one of the original members of the Oxford Movement, was the one who did most to establish the doctrine of the Incarnation in the form that became most influential and contributed toward the socialization of the Oxford Movement and of Anglo-Catholic spirituality. Wilberforce had himself been influenced by John Adam Moehler, the Roman Catholic theologian at Munich. Moehler's *Symbolik* (1832) applied "to the Church in a special manner the Hegelian doctrine . . . of Incarnation as an eternal fact, of collective humanity as the perpetual manifestation of the life of God."[28] In his book on *The Doctrine of the Incarnation* (1848), Wilberforce cited Moehler and in his conclusion looked out upon a world that was crumbling and could not be saved, believing that the crumbling "elements of order cannot readjust themselves save by reference to the natural law of their being." The saving "principle" based on love rather than on force, is to be found only "in that power whereby nature is elevated above itself," that is, in Christ, "the Pattern and representative of our being, the New Man, the second Adam of redeemed mortality." The Incarnate One reveals the law of our being, preaching "humility in the palace and self-respect in the lowly hovels of the poor," enforcing "such lessons of self-denial as may mitigate the glare of earthly splendour, and demonstrating to philosophy the existence of a law above its reach."[29]

Such an understanding was to be further developed until in the Anglo-Catholic symposium, *Lux Mundi* (1889), J. K. Illingsworth could write:

> "The Incarnation opened heaven, for it was the revelation of the Word; but it also re-consecrated earth, for the Word was made Flesh and dwelt among us. And it is impossible to read history without feeling how profoundly the religion of the Incarnation has been a religion of humanity. The human body itself, which heathendom had so degraded that noble minds could only view it as the enemy and prison of the soul, acquired a new meaning, exhibited new graces, shone with a new lustre in the light of the Word made Flesh; and thence, in widening circles, the family, society, the state itself felt in their turn the impulse of the Christian spirit with its

'Touches of things common,
Till they rose to touch the spheres.' "[30]

Here was the basis for social reform and for Catholic humanism.
The world and its inhabitants were not to be despised but to be
cared for after the pattern of the Incarnate One.

Such thought was akin to much in Coleridge and reflected the
conviction of F. D. Maurice that in Christ the radical distinction between the sacred and the secular was overcome. To Maurice, the
church is "human society in its normal state; the World that same
society irregular and abnormal. The World is the Church without
God; the Church is the World taken back by Him into the state for
which he created it."[31] Maurice's theology influenced *Lux Mundi*
and Anglo-Catholicism, contributing toward the critical change
from other-worldliness to an incarnational view of the world with
serious implications for societal reform.[32] We turn now, then, to
Maurice.

F. D. Maurice: Spirituality Grounded in the Universal Law of Sacrifice

Frederick Denison Maurice (1805-1872) was Chaplain of
Lincoln's Inn at the Inns of Court in London, a professor at King's
College, London, and subsequently professor of Moral Theology
and Moral Philosophy at Cambridge University. He is
remembered as a founder and the "prophet" of the Christian
Socialist Movement and as one of the most influential theologians
of his day, his influence extending to the United States during the
latter part of the nineteenth century and on into the twentieth.[33]
That influence effected the spirituality of many for it sprang from a
deep, pervasive spirituality.[34]

There are different ways of approaching an understanding of
Maurice's spirituality. We may begin with the question posed by
Maurice: "What is the true nature of humanity?" He answered
saying that contrary to the opinion of many, humanity is not
fundamentally evil. Beneath evil there is righteousness—such
righteousness as every human being senses as the deepest truth
about herself or himself.[35] That underlying righteousness is not an
abstraction but a Person: the pre-existent, indwelling Christ.
"Apart from Him, I feel that there dwells in me no good thing; but
I am sure that I am not apart from Him, nor are you, nor is any
man."[36] "Christ is the Head of everyman, whether that fact is

acknowledged or not."[37] Maurice's conviction is derived in part
from the Johannine affirmation that Christ is "the light that en-
lightens every man."[38] The perception of this undergirding, personal righteousness is the work of reason, reason which is not
merely an organizing or synthesizing function of the mind. Reason
liberates us from the confines of the mind, and from our feelings
as well, in order that we may perceive that which is the ground of
our being. Reason is "conversant with that which is universal as
well as with that which is necessary."[39]

On the basis of this understanding of humanity there follows the
realization that we are members of a species or kind (collective
humanity) whose fundamental law is revealed by Christ to be that
of sacrifice, not selfishness.[40] Maurice's spirituality involves
recognition that we are social creatures, members of a species,
living under the law that governs our kind. "Kindness and
Gentleness cease where there is no sense of a Kind or Gens. They
grow with the growth of that sense . . . A creature sinking into itself dies; so long as it is associated with a kind, it lives."[41]

In a sermon preached at Lincoln's Inn in 1854, Maurice dwells
on sacrifice as being the law of human kind. Christ's significance,
Incarnate as Man rather than simply a man, was that he lived out
"the law of kind." He thus revealed, as Paul understood in Phil.
2:5-12, "that in obedience, humiliation, sacrifice, dwelt the
mighty conquering power."[42] Indeed, wherever we see "humiliation, and obedience, and sacrifice" whether it be in a Christian, a
Muslim, or some other, we see the evidence of righteousness, of
Christ in that person, and of the fruits of the Incarnation.

> "Go through the history of the world, of the Church, of individuals,
> you will find it the same. So long as you creep along the ground,
> and ask why this man, or this party, or this faith, overcame, and
> that was subdued, you may be continually disposed to doubt and
> arraign the Providence that directs all things, to charge God fool-
> ishly. But ascend above the mists of earth to the clear heavens
> where Christ sits at the right hand of God, and the eternal law
> becomes manifest which brings these discords into harmony. The
> Will that rules the universe, the Will that has triumphed and does
> triumph, is all expressed and gathered up in *the Lamb that was
> slain*. Beholding Him, you see whence comes its confusion. The
> principle of sacrifice has been ascertained once and for ever to be
> *the* principle, the divine principle; that in which God can alone fully
> manifest His own eternal Being, His inmost character, the order
> which He has appointed all creatures, voluntarily or involuntarily,
> to obey."[43]

Christ is at the center of Maurice's spirituality, the Incarnate Son of God, who through humbling Himself to be born, live and die among us, revealed the true nature of our human being. To acknowledge the law of sacrifice as the law of our kind and to live by it is to become fully human. To acknowledge that law not as abstract but as a Person, Christ Jesus, who suffered death upon the Cross and by His sacrifice saved all people, is to be a member of the Church. In the light of this revelation Maurice viewed all else, including personal and corporate worship and the social implications of the Gospel.

When speaking of personal prayer he had sacrifice in mind. In 1860 he wrote that if prayers

"are separated from the confession and presentation of the perfect Sacrifice, once made—if they are not petitions that the will which is expressed in that sacrifice may be done on earth as it is in Heaven, if they are not presented through the High Priest and Mediator within the veil—they are, in my judgment, not Christian prayers."[44]

It was thus important that when setting about to pray we recognize who it is to whom we are praying and through whom. The opening of the Lord's Prayer provides the essential direction. We are to pray "Hallowed be Thy Name": that prayer sets the tone. For God's Name has been hallowed in the Old Israel and in the New, "by individual trials," by prophets and saints, by every baptism and holy communion, by the life and death of Christ, and by the faith of the dying. That prayer, "Hallowed be Thy Name." has been answered and "will be answered when we all yield ourselves up in deed and in truth to the Spirit of God, that we like our Lord may glorify His Name upon the earth, and may accomplish the work that He has given us to do."[45] The approach to God in prayer thus involves a daily oblation of ourselves, our souls and bodies, the self sacrifice that involves confession.

Maurice had a lively awareness of the reality of sin. All have been set free from sin "by the blood of Christ," but all abide in sin "inspite of Christ's redemption."[46] Therefore prayer to God must at the outset be the prayer of confession, sincere confession of personal and corporate guilt. That which hinders us from sincere prayer is that which hinders us from relationship with God, from acknowledging and living by the law of our kind. Through daily confession we are "put in the way of humbling our own lofty looks, of laying low our haughtiness, of exalting the Lord alone."[47] That is to say, in confession, by God's grace, we turn from selfishness to sacrifice, from inhumanity to humaneness, from unrighteousness to righteousness, acknowledging what has been done for us and all people in Christ and what Christ is doing in us now. This approach to prayer then affects all our subsequent prayer and praise. For instance, we pray as the Lord commanded us to do for daily bread, but our prayer is not for unlimited wealth, it is prayer for only that which is needed to sustain us. "Bread for subsistence will not under any circumstances, be bread for mere display, for waste, for rivalry."[48] If we needed any further evidence for the fact that Maurice's fundamental principle, the principle of the universe, extends into social policy, there is that further evidence here. To live by the law of sacrifice is to live in such a way that the self is not dominated by greed and gluttony but is active receiving and giving as Christ received and gave, sacrificially.

Maurice was deeply appreciative of the corporate worship of the church and rejoiced in the fact that the Church of England placed corporate worship, including sacraments, before doctrine. The *Book of Common Prayer* was proof of this. Furthermore its inclusiveness provided a preventative against "narrowness and sectarianism."[49] In essence the Prayer Book was the bond of unity of both Church and Nation. It was not perfect, but he claimed, "it has helped me to see more of the love of God and of the bonds by which men are knit to each other, and to feel more hope as to those whom I should naturally regard as foes, than any other book except the Bible."[50] When considering Mattins he argued that "the merit of any particular forms [of prayer] will consist very much in the degree in which they educate men out of their natural inclination to bury themselves in a set of partial, selfish interests and awaken them to a consciousness of common position and privileges."[51] Morning Prayer begins with confession and thus at the outset draws the worshipper "out of the individualism which is our curse and ruin, and leads us, one and all, to take up our position on the same ground of being justified and redeemed in Christ."[52]

Baptism was for Maurice "the sacrament of constant union."[53] The work of the Holy Spirit in the sacrament is to "bring people out of separation into union with God. In addition to asserting man's union with God on the ground of the forgiveness of his sins,

Baptism is also the sacrament of constant union with the whole people of God."[54] Infant baptism is explained in terms of the objective character of Christ's sacrifice for all people, without regard to their faith or morals. It thus proclaims: "that there is a constant union between Christ and the human race, that the ground of human community is such unity, and that the ultimate basis of God's union with man and of men with themselves is the Unity of the Holy Trinity."[55] Maurice regarded the Holy Communion as the powerful rehearsal of God's mightiest act on behalf of humanity, a drama far more effective than any words. He explains his meaning in speaking of what Christians should tell those living in ignorance of God's saving act in and through Christ.

> "We shall tell them that a living and perpetual communion has been established between God and man; between earth and heaven; between all spiritual creatures: that the bond of this communion is that body and blood which the Son of God and the Son of Man offered up to His Father, in fulfilment of His Will, in manifestation of His love; that God is as careful to nourish their spirits as their bodies; that as He provides bread and wine for the strength and life of the one, so in this body and blood of His Son is the strength of the other; the Sacrament of His continual presence with His universal family; the witness to each man of his own place in that family, and of his share in all its blessings; the pledge and spring of a renewed life; the assurance that this life is his own eternal life."[56]

One could go on to show how Maurice's spirituality, the spirituality of sacrifice, effected his involvement in the life and struggles of his time. With his perception of sacrifice as the law of the universe it is not surprising that he tended to condemn capitalism and applaud socialism, but he was not blind to the faults of socialism, believing as he did that it desperately needed to be Christianized. It is not surprising that he advocated cooperation over competition and was willing to invest time and energy in the cooperative movement of his day. He was not without faults, but he did set forth in vivid terms for the modern world the secret of its salvation and of its destruction. In doing so he proved himself to be a continuator of the best in Christianity and in Anglican tradition. F. D. Maurice was a man of prayer. He prayed fervently. Some of his most learned admirers have been at a loss to understand the depths of his piety, the hours spent on his knees praying, the agony he knew along with the joy. Such devotion is under-

standable when we realize how steadily his attention was fixed
upon the Incarnate, the Lamb that was slain, the One offered,
sacrificed upon the Cross for us to reveal to us the law of our kind
and gens and to inspire in us kindness and gentleness.

William Temple: Life as Constant Fellowship with God

We have seen something of William Temple's spirituality in the
sermon on sacrifice preached at Repton in 1918. There we found
him emphasizing the Person of Christ calling us to sacrifice and
thus to realize our true nature in Him. Implicit in this understanding
is the Incarnation of God in Christ, for when we look to Christ we
behold God.[57] In Christ God is revealed as love, not as doctrine
"but as its very image." In a powerful passage found in *Christus
Veritas*, Temple continues:

> "We are not left to conceive the all-embracing love of God as a
> general idea; we can call to mind the Agony and the Cross. There
> we see what selfishness in us means to God; and if evil means that
> to God, then God is not indifferent to evil. He displays His utter
> alienation from evil by showing us the pain that it inflicts on Him.
> So more than in any other way He rouses us from acquiescence in
> our own selfishness. By His refusal to discriminate in His Love, and
> His surrender of Himself for men's evil passions to torment, He
> wins us to deserve His love and kills the evil passions in a degree
> that would be impossible by any activity of righteous force."[58]

If in our self-complacency we inhibit the appeal of that love or
prevent it from reaching our hearts, God allows our selfishness to
work its woe. He takes no delight in human suffering, but in love
God lets the pain of sin work to humble us, opening us at last to
admit His love into our hearts, thus to transform us from death to
life. The aim of the Christian life is fellowship with God, "fellowship with Love—utter, self-forgetful and self-giving love."[59]
Salvation "consists in the substitution of the Spirit of the Whole for
the spirit of the particular self in the control of all life—conduct,
thought, feeling." Only as we submit to the Universal Spirit, God's
Spirit, for the direction of our lives, can we truly love as we are
meant to love. Temple states that:

> "love itself is self-centered, and leads to a group egoism as
> dangerous as individual selfishness, unless it is either love of God or
> rooted in love of God. The mother who is utterly devoted to her

children may be possessed by an intense family-selfishness. Even for the salvation of love we depend on the power of the self-manifested love of God to draw us into fellowship with itself by eliciting an answering love. But if in answer to God's love I begin to love Him, my love for Him must make me, for His sake, love those whom He loves as He loves me. To love God, as He is revealed in Christ, prevents all malice or envy or contempt, so far as it influences us at all, and redeems our very love from selfishness."[60]

The Christian life is a life lived in constant fellowship with God. The focus is on God and thus it is also on prayer, but in accordance with his basic premise prayer, and worship as a whole, is the totality of Christian life involving what we do as well as what we say to God. "Worship includes all life, and [those] moments spent in concentrated worship, whether 'in Church' or elsewhere, are the focussing points of the sustaining and directing energy of the worshipper's whole life."[61] Prayer is a means by which fellowship with God, and with God's people, is maintained. As Christians we are involved with others. "The Christian life is a life of membership in a society."[62] It is most definitely not a purely personal affair. The Lord's Prayer expresses our involvement with one another in fellowship with God. We pray "*Our* Father," "Give *us* our daily bread." We are all children of God, members of one family. Our intercessory prayers, when they are done in the right spirit, acknowledge our primary fellowship with God and with one another in God. Temple wrote:

"Prayer is an expression of love. Where there is no love, there can be no prayer. Sometimes the love may be very feeble, and only strong enough to give rise to a real prayer; yet if we make that prayer, it will strengthen the love it springs from, as an expression of an emotion tends to strengthen that emotion. And so a better prayer becomes possible. Prayer and love deepen each other. If we are Christians in any living sense, our love is sure to find expression in prayer, and so to become deeper. Prayer, therefore, and especially mutual intercession, is one great means of increasing the volume of love in the world."[63]

That is to say, by consciously praying the activities of God are released in the world, strengthening the character of our entire lives, lives which are then indeed prayers, the most complete worship of God, and the fullest expression of divine love. "God is love; and the love from which prayer springs is the Holy Ghost at work in our hearts."[64]

At the heart of worship for Temple there were the sacraments, and in particular the Eucharist. It was his conviction that "the act of worship . . . like all other human acts, must at least have physical expression, and is so far always sacramental."[65] Temple, grounded as he was in the doctrine of the Incarnation, was a sacramentalist. As Joseph Fletcher says, "To him the sacramental process is the dialectic of spirit and matter. He spoke often of 'the ethical utilization of a material object for a spiritual end,' and called a sacrament 'the embodiment of spiritual things.'"[66] The use of water in baptism expresses physically "the cleansing from the effect of worldly influence (which is Original Sin) so that heavenly influence may do its perfect work." Baptism also involves "incorporation into the Church (or into Christ). These are not two things, but one. It is through the Church that the influence of Christ reaches us."[67] "The Church itself is a sacrament of human nature indwelt by God; to become a member of the Church is to become a participator in human nature so indwelt."[68] The point is that through Baptism one comes under or into the influence of Love and being imbued with the Holy Spirit begins to experience the effects of that influence in a turning away from selfishness to self-giving.

The Eucharist is the dramatic representation of the action of Christ at the heart of the Last Supper. There Christ said, "This is my Body." "Do this." These words are repeated at every Eucharist. What do they mean? At the Last Supper they must have meant, "As I treat this Bread, so I treat my Body; and you must do the same." The sacrificial nature of the language assisted the disciples in understanding that Christ's death on the next day was to be the one true sacrifice, the end of all sacrifices. But that sacrifice was not limited to the Cross. It involved the totality of Christ's obedience and through Him the obedience of humanity, for which the Cross is the supreme symbol. That union of Christ with humanity in obedience resulted in a new society, the Church. And thus in the Eucharist,

> "which is pre-eminently the Christian's means of access to the Eternal, and wherein he worships not as an individual but as a member of the Church of all times and places, the relevant conception of Christ is not that of the historic Figure but that of the Universal Man. The sacrifice of Christ is potentially but most really the sacrifice of Humanity. Our task is, by His spirit, to take our place in that sacrifice. In the strict sense there is only one

sacrifice—the obedience of the Son to the Father, and of Humanity to the Father in the Son. This was manifest in actual achievement on Calvary; it is represented in the breaking of the Bread; it is re-produced in our self-dedication and resultant service; it is consummated in the final coming of the Kingdom."[69]

Here is the locus, the critical point for the development of Christian spirituality, where the individual human being in the fellowship of the Church reaches through in worship to the God made manifest in Christ, the Lamb sacrificed for us. We see the Lamb that was slain in the breaking of the Bread. We respond as the Spirit empowers us with the offering of our selves, our souls and bodies for service to God and to God's mission in the world. And we do this in the knowledge of the future hope, that the sacri-fice on the cross, represented in the breaking of the Bread and reproduced in the sacrifice and sacrificial service, will be con-summated "in the final coming of the Kingdom." Those who worship in and through the Eucharist are maintained in that fellowship with God begun in baptism, and become daily more fully the instruments of divine love in the world. The devotional and the social aspect of Christian life are one. "Worship includes all life."

Temple suggests that we usually think of the Eucharist in terms of redemption and argues that we should also think of it in relation to creation if we would realize the full impact of the sacrament on contemporary society. The bread and wine are impressive symbols of economic life, for in order to have bread, land must be cultivated, grain scattered and in time harvested, flour produced and baked. Prior to that process, however, there must be that which only God can give: life, soil, sun and rain. The same can be said of the wine. Bread and wine, the elements of the Eucharist, necessitate cooperation between God and humanity.

"In the Holy Communion service we take the bread and wine—man's industrial and commercial life in symbol—and offer it to God; because we have offered it to Him, He gives it back to us as a means of nurturing us, not in our animal nature alone, but as agents of His purpose, limbs of a body responsive to His will; and as we receive it back from Him, we share it with one another in true fellowship. If we think of the service in this way, it is a perfect picture of what secular society ought to be; and a Christian civili-zation is one where the citizens seek to make their ordered life something of which that service is the symbol."[70]

This is not the place to examine Temple's social principles in detail. It is sufficient, having noted his intense involvement in the social issues of his day, that such involvement was a necessary part of spirituality for him. Writing of his primary social principles, Temple spoke of God and His purpose, which is to win society out of "a welter of competing selfishness" into "a fellowship of love." This he did: "He came on earth and lived out the divine love in human life and death. He is increasingly drawing men to Himself by the love thus shown."[71] The second primary principle has to do with humanity, its dignity, tragedy and destiny. Here he says:

> "Man is self-centred; but he always carries with him abundant proof that this is not the real truth of his nature. He has to his credit both capacities and achievements that could never be derived from self-interest. The image of God—the image of holiness and love—is still there, though defaced; it is the source of his aspirations; it is even—through its defacement—the occasion of his perversity. It is capable of response to the Divine Image in its perfection if ever this can be presented to it. This is the glory of the Gospel. It enables man to see 'the light of the knowledge of the glory of God in the face of Jesus Christ,' and so 'with veiled face, reflecting as a mirror the glory of the Lord,' man may be 'transformed into the same image from glory to glory.' "[72]

In addition to these primary principles, Temple specified three derivative principles for Christian social action, but also for the guidance of society whether Christian or not. The first is freedom to make deliberate choices. Society must do all in its power to guard and not stifle that freedom. The second principle concerns human need for society, for fellowship: "By our mutual influence we actually constitute one another as what we are."[73] Consequently everything possible must be done to cultivate fellowship not only on the level of the state or national community but in those intermediate communities extending from family groupings to schools, professional associations, city organization, the Churches and the like. Human beings not only have the right to fellowship, they die without it. The third derivative principle is that of service. As freedom and fellowship are necessary, so is service, for service is the obligation of all who enjoy freedom and fellowship. Here Temple has in mind the theological doctrine of sacrifice but puts it in rather ordinary terms. If we are to be truly human we will be guided in our policy and in our careers by the principles of service, letting our wider loyalties check our narrower.

"A man is a member of his family, of his nation, and of mankind. It is very seldom that anyone can render a service directly to mankind as a whole. We serve mankind by serving those parts of it with which we are closely connected. And our narrower loyalties are likely to be more intense than the wider and therefore call out more devotion and more strenuous effort. But we can and should check these keener, narrower loyalties by recognizing the prior claim of the wider."[74]

Spirituality for Temple includes the struggle, sometimes against great odds, to apply in both personal and social existence the principles of freedom, fellowship and service as derived from the more fundamental principles of God's purpose and our destiny. To live by such principles the Christian needs to be maintained in constant fellowship with God and is so maintained by the all-embracing love of God demonstrated once for all in the Agony and on the Cross.

Evelyn Underhill: Life as Adoration, Communion and Cooperation

Evelyn Underhill (1875-1941) first gained public attention as a scholar and a person of keen spiritual insight with the publication of *Mysticism* in 1911. Her life story is in part the tale of her pilgrimage from mysticism without any specific Christian content to a discovery of the centrality of Christ, his Incarnation and Sacrifice, membership in the Church of England, and the publication of another scholarly work, representative of her new insights, called *Worship*, in 1936. Instrumental in her conversion was the famed Baron von Hugel. He it was who helped her to open her eyes, mind and heart to Christ, becoming for a time her friend and spiritual director. In her mature years she was much in demand as a retreat leader, her devotional writings were hailed as practical, down to earth, and yet capable of inspiring their readers to new visions of the spiritual life, and she was looked upon increasingly as one who provided a meaningful bridge between the spiritual wisdom of the ancients and the deepest perceptions not only of twentieth century spiritual leaders but also of psychologists, physicists, and the like. Of all those we have considered thus far

Evelyn Underhill comes closest to being a professional expert on
Christian spirituality—a description that she quite rightly would
have abhorred.
How did she understand the Christian life? Underhill explained
her views so often and so variously that it is difficult to know
where to begin. Just a year after she went to Baron von Hugel in
1921 for spiritual direction, she wrote of the three chief ways in
which humans perceive the real, the eternal, the divine—the
transcendent Other—three types of spiritual awareness:

> "The cosmic, ontological, or transcendent; finding God as the
> infinite Reality outside and beyond us. The personal, finding Him
> as the living and responsive object of our love, in immediate touch
> with us. The dynamic, finding Him as the power that dwells within
> or energizes us. These are not exclusive but complementary appre-
> hensions, giving objectives to intellect, feeling and will. They must
> all be taken into account in any attempt to estimate the full
> character of the spiritual life, and thus life can hardly achieve per-
> fection unless all three be present in some measure."[75]

It is not surprising that in the next step she sees in the three ways
the Trinity, the doctrine of the Trinity being "above all the crystal-
lization and mind's interpretation of these three ways in which our
simple contact with God is actualized by us."[76] She goes further to
suggest that the first moment of the spiritual life consists of our
apprehension of "Eternal Life." The second, without which the
first is virtually worthless, consists of our "response to that transcendent Reality." Thirdly, to perceive that Reality is to be obliged
to live "in its atmosphere, fulfilling its meaning" if we can and this
in turn involves "a measure of inward transformation, a difficult
growth and change."

> "Thus the ideas of new birth and regeneration have always been,
> and I think must ever be, closely associated with man's discovery of
> God: and the soul's true path seen to be from intuition, through
> adoration, to moral effort, and thence to charity."[77]

Another way of putting it, one that clearly shows the influence
of Olier, who founded the Paris Oratory in the seventeenth
century, is to say that the basic ingredients of Christian spirituality
are adoration, communion and cooperation. Adoration is the first
step in self-transcendence, the necessary preliminary to
petitionary prayer, as the Lord's Prayer indicates. Adoration is

"the response 'of awe-struck love' to the overshadowing Reality of God, the 'first real response of the awakened creature.' "[78] Communion is prayer. Prayer has at its heart adoration but the object of adoration is not distant; God is near and indeed can be said to be "the medium in which man lives and moves and has his being."[79]

"In the last analysis, communion is both God acting and man acting, for communion is essentially both putting on Christ and receiving his light. It is thanks to communion with God in Christ that human life is transformed into a focus of divine presence and power in the world. Moulded by the Spirit in prayerful communion both priest and teacher for instance can hand on the 'contagion' of God—not otherwise."[80]

Through adoration the transcendent is acknowledged, through communion the immanent presence of God is experienced, and both reach out for completion in cooperation, divine action in and through the self-abandoned worshipper. For Underhill action is a part of and the fulfillment of prayer. Thus she wrote:

"The final purification in love of the human spirit, and the full achievement of its peculiar destiny as a collaborator in the Spirit's work, must go together: obverse and reverse of the unitive life. Then the soul's total prayer enters and is absorbed into, that ceaseless Divine action by which the created order is maintained and transformed. For by the prayer of self-abandonment, she enters another region; and by adherence is established in it. There the strange energy of will that is in us and so often wasted on unworthy ends, can be applied for the world's needs—sometimes in particular actions, sometimes by absorption into the pure act of God."[81]

The achievement of this end through self-abandonment was not to be sought in any "method"; here she parted company with other theologians of the spiritual life. She preferred "programme" to "method" believing that the way or ways must be kept flexible, that that is worthwhile which is workable for particular people in their place and time. The "programme" must somehow be creative in providing "the atmosphere of God." That is the all important consideration. As she wrote in 1927, reflecting on her conversion, she attended Holy Communion in the Church of England at first as a matter of obedience, but then she gradually became aware of its becoming "more and more wonderful . . . It's in that world and atmosphere one lives."[82] It is in living in "the atmosphere of God" abandoned to the working of the Spirit that the dualism between this world and the other world fades. Underhill was constantly concerned to stress that the distinction between the spiritual life and the practical life was false: "Most of our conflicts and difficulties come from trying to deal with the spiritual and practical aspects of our life separately instead of realizing them as parts of a whole."[83] Much of her effort in retreats was expended in helping people to realize the essential wholeness of their lives.

Self-abandonment was obviously central to Underhill's understanding of Christian spirituality and must be understood in relation to the doctrine of sacrifice. Furthermore, our worship must be understood as a means towards that sacrifice which is self-abandonment. As she said: "Worship, the response of the human creature to the Divine, is summed up in sacrifice; the action which expresses more fully than any other his deep if uncomprehended relation to God."[84] In her discussion of worship her attention is fixed on the Cross. She acknowledges sacrifice as something fundamental in humans, coming from the jungle, first expressed in primitive sacrificial rites.

> "But its full meaning is disclosed in the absolute oblation of the Cross. Cost is always essential to it. Thus wild animals and fruits are never used by agricultural peoples for the purposes of sacrifice. They must give something into which they have put their own life and work; for within that total, visible offering which is ritual sacrifice, is always implied the total invisible offering of the self, and everything the self best loves."[85]

In the Cross, as seen together with the Last Supper and the Agony of Gethsemane, the full meaning of sacrifice is revealed. "Life is offered, and being offered is transformed in God: and by and through this life given and transformed, God enters into communion with men."[86] Here salvation is worked, revealing to us the key to the meaning of life, the reality that communion with the divine life can only occur with the surrender of what is only apparently life. Underhill concludes:

> "And when the interior life of prayer is reached—that life on which, in the last resort, the reality of the cultus must depend—those three great motives of sacrifice which the ancient rituals express: the deep

sense of sin and penitence, the need and longing for communion, the impulse to that total self-giving which is the preparation of sanctity—are all found operative in the most profound experiences of the soul."[87]

Here again we have the three ways, the three basic ingredients of the spiritual life, for it is in apprehending the transcendent, adoring the righteous God, that we know our sin and are made penitent. It is in the revelation that the transcendent is personal, "the living and responsive object of our love," that in Christ we are brought into communion with God, that we know ourselves to be forgiven. God in Christ is very near to us, within us, enlivening us, to give over ourselves in response to Christ's sacrifice, giving ourselves over to the divine action working in and through us. This is the work of the Holy Spirit moving us to live lives of sacrificial service.

In the end, Underhill has a lively sense of spirituality as issuing in action. As she puts it, "Man does not truly love the Perfect until he is driven thus to seek its incarnation in the world of time."[88] But she is wary, realizing that many involved in the so-called Social Gospel movement were ignorant of and cared not at all for what she understands to be the spiritual life. Her judgment is that, "Without the inner life of prayer and meditation, lived for its own sake and for no utilitarian motive, neither our judgments upon the social order nor our active social service will be perfectly performed; because they will not be the channel of Creative Spirit expressing itself through us in the world to-day."[89] The ideal, as she perceives it, involves striking a balance:

"First, a personal contact with Eternal Reality, deepening, illuminating and enlarging all of our experience of fact, all our responses to it: that is, faith. Next, the fullest possible membership of and duty towards the social organism, a completely rich, various, heroic, self-giving, social life: that is, charity. The dissociation of these two sides of human experience is fatal to that divine hope which should crown and unite them; and which represents the human instinct for novelty in a sublimated form."[90]

This is no more and no less than we have encountered all the way in this journey from the nineteenth to the twentieth century. The beginning is in encounter with God from whom comes the impetus and the direction for the deepest involvement in the affairs of this world.

Conclusion

We have surveyed the thought of Anglicans from Wilberforce to Temple on the subject of Christian spirituality. As was suggested at the outset, this presentation is not definitive. Many important people and points of view have been omitted. In a sense our quest has been for an understanding of the worldly/other-worldly dichotomy. The trend in modern Anglicanism, as Temple pointed out, has been from the other-worldliness of the early nineteenth century Evangelicals to the this-worldly concerns of the Christian Socialists and Social Gospellers. Maurice attempted to overcome the separation of the sacred from the secular through an application of the doctrine of the Incarnation expressed in his slogan: "Christ in every man." We have noted how Underhill believed that living in "the atmosphere of God," abandoned to the working of the Spirit, the oppositions of worldly/other-worldly and spiritual life/practical life fade away. T. S. Eliot, whose *Four Quartets* has been read as a spiritual classic by many, referred to the universalized Incarnation as a moment in and out of time, the "point of intersection of the timeless/With time," and thus emphasized the overcoming of the worldly/other-worldly dichotomy. This intersection the poet experienced personally in moments of intense consciousness, moments he called "annunciations," and also in the holy routine of the church, its prayers in general and the Eucharist in particular. The annunciations are exceptional and seldom occur and then unexpectedly. The holy routine is always available to those who are themselves available. In this way Eliot speaks of the meeting of time and the timeless in such a way that their utter separation is denied but so also is their entire absorption in one or the other.[91]

There is in all of us a kind of instinct or drive that propels us on the quest for wholeness in the midst of chaos, a hunger and thirst that is only satisfied when we find the Ultimate incarnate in time. We have also noted—Temple and Underhill were especially at pains to make this point—that being limited as we are we cannot find that which we seek simply by immersion in time or in what is popularly called the secular world. This chapter has suggested that although there are serious dangers in other-worldliness there are also serious dangers in this-worldliness. To prevent being lost, wallowing in half-truths or falsehoods because they are all we know and can invest our lives in, we need to realize that the revelation which brings new life and wholeness comes to us from beyond ourselves, revealing the truth about our situation, calling and empowering us to transcend our limitations. For Anglicans and other Christians this revelation comes through the Gospel in the Scripture, received and interpreted by Tradition to spirit-filled Reason. It comes in Christ—in a Person—whose self-sacrifice draws from us the grateful response of sacrifice in worship and thus, too, in service.

There would seem to be a desperate need for balance, creative tension and dynamic interaction. Martin Thornton, who once based his theories of Christian spirituality on the foundations of Eric Mascall's theology and now adheres to the Christian existentialism of John Macquarrie, used the phrase "existential-ontological" as a key. The first word, "existential," emphasizes "human experience in the actual, concrete world, with its activity and movement, its anxiety, choice, potentiality, development and death."[92] By "ontological" he understands "the given, that which is set over against subjective experience; specifically the creed which contains revealed truths, those which I am most unlikely to have discovered or worked out for myself, which I accept in faith."[93] The two necessarily go together, balanced, in creative tension, with dynamic interaction. Having belabored the importance of the "existential" to the development of Christian spirituality, Thornton wants to emphasize that "experience alone, or a thoroughgoing empiricism, cannot form the basis of my religion."[94] We need "the given" if the necessary experience is to occur at all.

But what then of that which is revealed in "the given"? Ultimately the revelation that saves persons is personal. George Woods, chaplain of Downing College, Cambridge, in a painstaking exploration of *Theological Explanation* on the basis of empirical method, emphasized the personal and wrote of revelation as a personal act between persons. He accounted for the truth of the Christian message in terms of its being "established upon the truth about personal being in God and Man. Ultimate explanation cannot consist in affirming that God has acted unless we have some understanding of the meaning of the act and the character of the one who has acted."[95] That understanding is provided for in the personal revelation of God in Christ through the activity of the Spirit. But it must be received in such a way that it becomes our understanding. That is to say that Christian spirituality presumes a personal relationship with God and such a relationship requires

that we be open and available. Such openness and availability is
in part our work, the work of self-abandonment in Underhill's
terms, but it is ultimately "worked" by God. Word and Sacrament
are powerful, through their dramatic representation of the personal revelation of God in Christ, in drawing us into communion
with God and nurturing us through participation in Christ,
inspiring us to the practice of sacrificial love. Thomas Cranmer
understood this. The *Book of Common Prayer* was produced in
large part to facilitate personal participation in Christ as a means of
creating a society motivated by love rather than greed.[96]

As William Temple taught, Christianity concerns constant fellowship with God. That fellowship is the basis of Christian spirituality
and it is corporate, for being in constant fellowship with God
means participating in that human fellowship called into being by
God. Furthermore, as Maurice reminds us, we belong to one
another as members of a species, a kind, a gens. It is as members
of such a fellowship that we discover the law of our kind, for being
together requires mutual sacrifice. Christian spirituality concerns
realizing our full humanity after the pattern of Christ and thus it
concerns our existence as members of groups and societies. The
law of sacrifice is meant to guide us in all that we think, desire and
do as part of families, schools, businesses, factories, professions,
cities, nations, and as inhabitants of planet earth.

The question arises whether there is a method involved in the
cultivation of Christian spirituality. Evelyn Underhill rightly answers
in the negative, preferring to speak of a "programme," or the
"atmosphere of God." It would seem, on the basis of the examination we have made, that Christian spirituality consists of three
parts or elements. First, there is that which Owen Chadwick calls
"interiority," the source of the dynamic power in the Oxford
Movement. This is that which the Evangelicals pointed to when
speaking of conversion, that which Newman referred to when
telling of the invisible world encroaching on the visible. Maurice
spoke of "Christ in every man" and the law of sacrifice, Temple of
constant fellowship with God, and Underhill of cosmic-ontological
awareness. Secondly, there is the expression of interiority in
piety, formal worship, ritual and ceremonial, Word and Sacraments, and the corporate, nurturing activity of Christians gathered
as the church. This is that to which Underhill referred when
speaking of communion. Finally, there is the expression of interiority in service, in sacrificial love directed not only to others in

the church but to others in the world at large, for the alleviation of suffering and through social action to change the structures of society for the sake of human freedom, fellowship and service, as Temple said. This is the dynamic activity of the Holy Spirit; but we must remember, as John Macquarrie points out, that it is not confined to the church or to Christians.[97] Thus arranged the three elements seem to follow logically from first to last. And, indeed, Underhill arranges the three in a different mode, indicating priority. Adoration is first and leads to communion, while communion leads to cooperation. This corresponds to the order of the persons of the Trinity, Father, Son and Holy Spirit.

Evangelicals and Tractarians, F. D. Maurice, William Temple and Evelyn Underhill were all aware of the existence and vital importance of the three elements of the spiritual life and, although they might for the sake of clarity speak of them sequentially, they all acknowledged their interpenetration and interdependence. Thus if we are to draw the chief conclusion from this brief study it would be that Anglican spirituality consists of that interiority which is adoration of God, prayer which is communion with God, and sacrificial love towards neighbors and others. But we would be remiss if we did not add that for all of those we have encountered this spirituality was nurtured through a personal relationship with Christ in whom all divinity and all humanity meet. Temple exhorted his schoolboys to think of, hear, and obey their "Hero-Redeemer" who died for them that they might have the power—the power of sacrifice—"that can once more 'turn the world upside down.'" Maurice affirmed, "Apart from Him, I feel that there dwells in me no good thing; but I am sure that I am not apart from Him, nor are you, nor is any man," and when he thought of Christ he thought of how the Son of God revealed the law of the universe in the sacrifice on the cross. Evelyn Underhill testified that although deeply religious she was unfulfilled until Baron von Hugel helped her to open her eyes, mind and heart to Christ and find the heart of her spirituality in the realization that "it is thanks to communion with God in Christ that human life is transformed into a focus of divine presence and power in the world." The personal encounter with Christ has been all important for such Anglicans. In a powerful sermon Dr. Pusey, the great nineteenth century Tractarian spoke of God calling us and all humanity, not as to abstract truth, not as to a program, policy, or method, but rather to a Person: "He calleth thee to Himself, that

He may give Himself unto thee. He calleth thee to give up all which is not He, that He may give thee all which HE IS. He calleth thee to give thee His Likeness."[98]

Footnotes

[1] William Temple, *Fellowship with God* (London: Macmillan, 1930), p. 205.

[2] Ibid., pp. 207-208.

[3] Ibid., p. 213.

[4] Ibid., pp. 214-215.

[5] Ibid., pp. 217-218.

[6] Ibid., p. 218.

[7] John V. Taylor, *The Go-Between God* (London: SCM Press, 1972), pp. 18-19.

[8] Marcel, *Foi et Réalité* (Aubier: Editions Montaigne, 1967), p. 125; translated by Joe McCown, *Availability: Gabriel Marcel and the Phenomenology of Human Openness* (Missoula, Montana: Scholars Press, n.d.), p. 20.

[9] For Cranmer, see his *Works*, ed. J. E. Cox, Parker Society (Cambridge, 1844-46), 1:42-43, 70-71, 271, etc., as well as the *Book of Common Prayer*, especially the Holy Communion; for Hooker see his *Of the Laws of Ecclesiastical Polity*, especially V. 56; and for Andrewes, see the *Collected Edition* of his works, espec. vol 1 (Oxford, 1841), p. 381.

[10] William Romaine, *The Life, Walk, and Triumph of Faith*, new ed. (London, 1856), pp. 20-21.

[11] Ibid., p. 481.

[12] I have been much indebted here to the insights of Ian Bradley, *The Call to Seriousness* (London: J. Cape, 1976).

[13] Hannah More, *Estimate of the Religion of the Fashionable World* (London: 1809), pp. 262-263.

[14] See Charles Smyth, *Simeon and Church Order* (Cambridge University Press, 1940), Ch. 1, espec. p. 22.

[15] Horton Davies, *Worship and Theology in England*, Vol. 3 (Princeton, N.J., Princeton University Press, 1961), p. 217.

[16] Charles Simeon, *The Excellency of the Liturgy* (New York, 1813), p. 79.

[17] Ibid., p. 91.

[18] Ibid., p. 103.

[19] Margaret Cropper, *Sparks Among the Stubble* (London: Longmans, Green, 1955), pp. 171-172.

[20] Georgina Battiscombe, *Shaftesbury* (Boston: Houghton Mifflin, 1975), p. 102.

[21] Basil Willey, *Nineteenth Century Studies* (New York: Columbia, 1950), pp. 76-77.

[22] J. H. Newman, *Parochial and Plain Sermons* (Oxford, 1834-42), 4:200-213.

[23] E. B. Pusey, *Sermons during the Season from Advent to Whitsuntide* (London, 1848), p. 299-300.

[24] Owen Chadwick, *The Mind of the Oxford Movement* (Stanford, California: Stanford University Press, 1967), p. 55.

[25] W. G. Ward, *Religion and Society in England, 1790-1850* (London: B. T. Batsford, Ltd., 1972), p. 235.

[26] Quoted from Newman's *Arians of the Fourth Century*, by William George Peck, *Social Implications of the Oxford Movement* (New York, London: C. Scribner's Sons, 1933), pp. 60-61.

[27] See Desmond Bowen, *The Idea of the Victorian Church* (Montreal: McGill University Press, 1968), pp. 287-288.

[28] Vernon Storr, *The Development of English Theology* (London: Longmans, Green, and Co., 1930), p. 262.

[29] R. I. Wilberforce, *The Doctrine of the Incarnation* (Philadelphia, 1849), pp. 410-411.

[30] Charles Gore, ed., *Lux Mundi: A Series of Studies in the Religion of the Incarnation*, from the 5th English ed. (New York: John Lovell Co., n.d.), p. 176.

[31] F. D. Maurice, *Theological Essays* (New York: Harper, 1957), pp. 276-77.

[32] For the social implications, see Maurice Reckitt, *From Maurice to Temple: A Century of Social Movement in the Church of England* (London: Faber and Faber, 1946).

[33] See William J. Wolf's essay on Maurice in *The Spirit of Anglicanism*, W. J. Wolf, ed. (Wilton, Conn.: Morehouse-Barlow Co., Inc., 1979), pp. 49-98.

[34] See the reports of his wife and his son concerning his practice of prayer in *The Life of Frederick Denison Maurice*, ed. by J. F. Maurice (New York: Charles Scribner's Sons, 1884), 2:285.

[35] Maurice, *Theological Essays*, pp. 54-67.

[36] Ibid., p. 67.

[37] *Life*, 1:154f.

[38] Maurice, *The Gospel of John* (London: Macmillan, 1857), pp. 100ff.

[39] Maurice, *The Kingdom of Christ* (London: Rivington, 1842), 1:166.

[40] See Maurice, *The Doctrine of Sacrifice* (London, 1893), pp. 312-313: "When it seems most, as if all acts and all events obeyed a law of selfishness, that law is really producing nothing, accomplishing nothing; it is merely intercepting, for a little while, by its feeble, insolent, vacillating rebellions, the calm, onward march of those armies which obey the true law of the universe, the law of sacrifice."

[41] Maurice, *Moral and Metaphysical Philosophy* (London, 1872), 1:xxvi.

[42] *The Doctrine of Sacrifice*, p. 219.

[43] Ibid., pp. 220-221; my emphasis.

[44] *Life*, 2:365.

[45] Maurice, *The Prayer Book . . . and the Lord's Prayer* (London, 1880), p. 303.

[46] *The Doctrine of Sacrifice*, pp. 284-85.

[47] *The Prayer Book*, p. 20.

[48] Ibid., p. 345.

[49] *Life*, 2:570.

[50] *Life*, 1:512.

[51] *Kingdom of Christ*, 2:229, quoted by Merlin Davies, *An Introduction to F. D. Maurice's Theology* (London: SPCK, 1964), p. 96.

[52] Ibid., p. 97.

[53] Alec Vidler, *Witness to the Light* (New York: Scribner's, 1948), p. 88.

[54] H. Davies, *Worship and Theology*, 3:307.

[55] Ibid., p. 308.

[56] *The Prayer Book*, pp. 230-231.

[57] On this, as well as on other matters of importance, see Owen Thomas' essay on Temple in *The Spirit of Anglicanism*, ed. Wolf, pp. 112ff.

[58] William Temple, *Christus Veritas* (London: Macmillan, 1949), p. 184.

[59] Ibid., p. 185.

[60] Ibid., pp. 221-222.

[61] Temple, *Citizen and Churchman* (London: Eyre and Spottiswoode, 1941), p. 101, quoted in Joseph Fletcher's *William Temple: Twentieth-Century Christian* (New York: Seabury Press, 1963), pp. 87-88.

[62] Temple, *Personal Religion and the Life of Fellowship* (London: Longmans, Green and Co., 1926), p. 36.

[63] Ibid., pp. 39-40.

[64] Ibid., p. 40.

[65] *Christus Veritas*, p. 232.

[66] Fletcher, *William Temple*, p. 92.

[67] *Christus Veritas*, pp. 236, 234.

[68] Ibid., p. 235.

[69] Ibid., pp. 238-239.

[70] Temple, *The Hope of a New World* (New York: Macmillan, 1943), p. 70.

[71] Temple, *Christianity and the Social Order* (London; SCM Press, 3rd. ed., 1950), p. 53.

[72] Ibid., pp. 57-58.

[73] Ibid., p. 63.

[74] Ibid., p. 70.

[75] Evelyn Underhill, *The Life of the Spirit and the Life of To-day* (New York: E. P. Dutton, 1922), pp. 13-14.

[76] Ibid., p. 14.

[77] Ibid., p. 15.

[78] Thus C. J. R. Armstrong in *Evelyn Underhill (1875-1941): An Introduction to her Life and Writings* (London and Oxford: Mowbrays, 1975), p. 269, citing *The Golden Sequence*, p. 158.

[79] Armstrong, ibid.

[80] Ibid., p. 270, citing *Collected Papers*, pp. 122-3, 189-90.

[81] Ibid., p. 271, quoting *The Golden Sequence*, pp. 182-3.

[82] Quoted by a Sister of the Society of St. Margaret in *Schools of Spirituality* (West Park, New York: Holy Cross Publications, 1967), p. 82.

[83] Armstrong, *Evelyn Underhill*, p. 273, quoting The Spiritual Life, p. 37.

[84] Underhill, *Worship* (New York: Harper and Brothers, 1937), p. 47.

[85] Ibid., p. 50.

[86] Ibid., p. 55.

[87] Ibid., p. 59.

[88] *The Life of the Spirit*, p. 267.

[89] Ibid., p. 268.

[90] Ibid., p. 271.

[91] See T. S. Eliot, *The Complete Poems and Plays* (New York: Harcourt, Brace and Co., 1952), pp. 136, 370-387.

[92] Martin Thornton, *Prayer: A New Encounter* (New York: Morehouse-Barlow, 1972), p. 41.

[93] Ibid., p. 46.

[94] Ibid., p. 45.

[95] G. F. Woods, *Theological Explanation* (Digswell Place, Welwyn: James Nisbet and Co., 1958), p. 210.

[96] John E. Booty, ed., *The Godly Kingdom of Tudor England: Great Books of the English Reformation* (Wilton, Conn.: Morehouse-Barlow, 1981), espec. chs. 1 and 3.

[97] John Macquarrie, *Paths in Spirituality* (New York: Harper and Row, 1972), p. 49.

[98] *The Mind of the Oxford Movement*, ed. O. Chadwick (Stanford, California: Stanford University Press, 1967), p. 158.

VI

The Spirituality of the
Book Of Common Prayer

Daniel B. Stevick

Public prayer in Anglicanism has, from the mid-sixteenth century, been shaped by one remarkable book. All churches are made what they are, in a great measure, by their distinctive ways of worship. But the Anglican ethos is peculiar in that so little else shares the central, formative, traditioning place that is occupied by the *Book of Common Prayer*. More than any other communion, Anglicanism has been constituted by its worship—and that means constituted, to a large extent, by one liturgical document: the English *Book of Common Prayer* and its now quite diverse progeny. In each church of the Anglican Communion, a Prayer Book is both officially authorized and freely and deeply loved. Any account of Anglican spirituality must give that book a primary place.

The Centrality of Worship

A group of churches which identifies and unifies itself around an authorized liturgy expresses a conviction that worship holds a central place in the Christian community. The church is not primarily a forum for thought and reflection; it is not primarily a league for mutual help, charitable works or social action. It may be all of those things rightly if, before and with all else, it is a community of acknowledgment, doxology and prayer.

The church describes itself in faith as a people summoned into being by the redemptive activity of God which centers in Jesus Christ. To use an old terminology, it is *congregatio* based on *convocatio*. God has set his love upon it; its distinctive life derives from its continued response to and participation in that ceaseless outgoing divine love. Thus the church's first business is with the God to whom it owes everything. Liturgy is a body of occasions through which the church both listens anew to that Word in which its life is constituted and offers the reply of confession, prayer and praise.

A rich liturgical life requires its rhythms of days and hours. But each act of worship is one moment set apart for the sake of every moment. Although worship articulates a dimension which pervades all of life, we cannot know the sacredness of all time unless that general, diffused meaning is given particular, concentrated expression. Thus the life of the church alternates between two forms: gathering for refreshment in Word and sacrament, and scattering for engagement in the world. And as with the collective life, so with the individual, each Christian moves between worship and work, the altar and the world.

Worship and mission—both of them rooted in Christ—are not in competition. Worship, for its integrity, needs to have brought to it the burden, struggle, joy and achievement of weekday Christian life. Without realistic engagement with the world, worship runs to aestheticism and risks becoming an inconsequential theatre of the sacred. But mission and service, without worship, run to activism or institution building. Our mindless, self-justifying busyness needs to be judged and redirected from that awed openness to the sovereign mystery of God which liturgy distinctively provides.

Theological discussion takes on a special character in a community whose unity is given by liturgy. Reflective discourse among Anglicans has not been shaped by an authoritative confession of faith, nor by a dominating theological mind, nor by pronouncements representing the church as official teacher. Rather, the quite diversified Anglican conversation on the meaning and implications of faith has been held together by a book whose common use has kept all participants in living engagement with the realities the theological discussion is all about—a book of prayer, praise, and community-making, community-sustaining sacramental actions. Discussion of ultimate reality in Anglicanism has not taken the form: How can my understanding conform to a statement which is taken to be a normative guide in such inquiry? Rather, it has taken the form (arguably a more intellectually exciting and religiously believable form): What must reality be like if we pray and praise in this way?

Prayer-talk does not presume to explain. It acknowledges; it celebrates; it presents. It frees the mind while at the same time it sets before the mind an urgent task. It can be rich, concrete and exact, according to its own character, and yet be open to a variety of constructions. Laudians and Latitudinarians, Evangelicals and Puseyites, mystics and social reformers, Christian Platonists,

Thomists and existentialists can all love and use loyally the *Book of Common Prayer* (Indeed, historically they all have done so.) while yet differing substantially as to what it means and requires.

One Liturgy: Many Spiritualities

When one speaks of "spirituality," one usually refers to a style of inner life and expression which characterizes a person or movement. One speaks of something more specific and personalized than the devotion of a large, catholic community can be. The Prayer Book was, in intention (although probably never fully successfully so), the liturgy of a nation at prayer. It was not meant to express a school of piety or a strongly marked personal vision. It urged no special techniques, and it proposed no novel vocabulary. It appealed to the Bible and the early church; it derived from the great, somewhat objective style of the Western liturgical tradition; and it was meant to be captive of no faction and acceptable to all. Thus the spiritualities of Anglicanism have been configurations, made by individuals or groups, of some of the life of devotion potentially opened by the Prayer Book. Persons with a definite style have loved and used the Prayer Book—all of the Prayer Book. Yet their expression has, so to speak, been "smaller" than the Prayer Book; or they have lived and believed within the spacious perimeter of the Prayer Book. The one official liturgy has encouraged, informed, contained, corrected and renewed many spiritualities. It would be misleading to speak of the *Book of Common Prayer* as though it were one type of Anglican spirituality alongside others. It is a powerful, comprehensive, authoritative influence whose character has shaped all Anglican spirituality in all generations. Its phrases, balance of themes, and its tone become internalized. Its qualities impart themselves to those who habitually and sympathetically use it.

Some Characteristics

The Prayer Book is what it is, of course, in part because of the historical situation in which it came to be. In speaking of the Prayer Book, Cranmer's name and intentions are mentioned repeatedly. But the work which took its shape in the sixteenth century has often been gratefully and creatively repossessed. The original drafters of the English Prayer Book did not set out to produce a devotional and liturgical classic or a monument of English prose. Their task was quite functional: to issue, in a rather short time for so large an undertaking, a serviceable, vernacular liturgical text for use throughout the reformed Church of England. They did their work with integrity, and they wrote better than they knew. Later generations have discovered qualities and depths in the Prayer Book that were doubtless unguessed and unintended by its compilers. The circumstances of its origin can account for the use of the Prayer Book in Tudor England. The fact that it has been validated as living prayer in subsequent generations and is still used (indeed, chosen and held in loyal affection) by a world-wide family of self-governing churches must be accounted for by the merits of the book itself. This book has qualities which let people discover and use it with a sense of deep fulfillment. It may be useful to explore what the Prayer Book can say in an age much different from that in which it was composed.

The following pages will consider several characteristics of the *Book of Common Prayer*—or perhaps more specifically, characteristics of the interaction between the Prayer Book and its users. In looking at each characteristic, two sorts of observations combine: on one level are matters of medium, function and style; on another are matters of the theology and spiritual discipline of Prayer Book worship. The two interpenetrate. In a work which has the greatness and wholeness of the *Book of Common Prayer*, issues of technique and issues of substance each imply something about the other.

1. Perhaps the most obvious thing to be observed about the Prayer Book is that *it is a book*. Its issuance coincided roughly with the beginning of the Gutenberg era. Anglican worship has been linked, since the sixteenth century, to a single book (that is to say, in addition to the Bible, a single book) of fairly handy size, which has been in the hands of officiants and congregation alike. Other Christian groups have, of course, used printed liturgical texts, but surely no other communion has in its public worship been so characteristically and continuously a "people of the book" as has Anglicanism.

Christian worship is not inherently wedded to the print medium. To look at the matter historically, prior to the sixteenth century, liturgical texts were carried by handwritten books and were therefore familiar as working documents largely to officiants in parish churches and monastic communities. To regress historically and look behind the Medieval service books, Christian worship in the earliest generations of the church used no written texts at all, except for biblical readings and Psalms. Yet the worship was not unformed. As in Jewish practice, the readings and Psalms followed definite progression; the prayers had order and sequence; and the congregations knew acclamations, responses and canticles. Prayer texts, when they began to be written out, were meant as a help for relatively ungifted officiants. The normal medium of liturgy was the oral/aural.

It still is. Prayer and praise are acts. They are brought into being by the living voice of speech or song. Any written text which is used is something like a prompt sheet which exists for the sake of the speaking and listening which it may make possible. But since Anglicans regularly use such a prompt sheet in worship, the relation of a Prayer Book to living prayer deserves further attention.

Reading and print are extremely complex phenomena. They create new modes of consciousness and communication; they make possible things that had not been possible before; and they make difficult some things that could previously be taken for granted. But even when print enters, liturgy remains rooted in the same fundamental medium in which consciousness itself is rooted: the miracle and mystery of speech. The race existed as fully human for millennia before writing, and later printing, were invented. Individually, as soon as we are born—long before we can read, write, or even speak—we are met by the rich flow of human talk. We come to an awareness of ourselves, of one another, and of our common world through the living exchange of language. For liturgy, as for life, later refinements—whether made possible by pen and paper, by movable type, or by vacuum tubes or silicon chips—may modify that basic human medium. But they do not displace it.

The experience of reading, especially silent reading, is an important factor in the development of one's consciousness. Through reading I come to know and name my inner life and I have access to a great resource from beyond myself. Reading is not universal, even in a literate society. It is not equally easy or rewarding for everyone and it is open to its own pitfalls, a false sort of "bookishness." But once a community or an individual has encountered reading, what one sees when attempting to look directly at nature or human life is strongly influenced by one's literary culture. Self-awareness and world-awareness open out together in this wonderful experience of taking in reality through the printed page.

Liturgy is prayer. It is act. Its medium is the spoken or sung word. Any prepared text that may be brought into worship has a kind of objectivity. Its specific qualities can be analysed by liturgical scholars or rhetoricians. But a liturgical text exists not primarily to be studied or admired, but for the sake of the vital, God-prompted, faith-filled worship which it may facilitate.

A parallel with music may be useful. Music exists as act in time; it is to be played or sung. To illustrate by one specific musical work, it is likely that Schubert never heard his String Quintet played. But since he worked it out in music notation and his musical intentions are recoverable, string players today can study the printed score, rehearse and then recreate the music. The silent score on the shelves of a music library is the indispensable precondition of performance. But the score exists for the sake of those fifty minutes or so when that glorious sound fills the hall.

2. Another characteristic, deriving from the foregoing, is the *givenness* of the *Book of Common Prayer*. It is there in the church pew before I arrive and open it—somewhat as the Schubert score stands on a shelf. It will be there when I leave. It preceded me and it will outlive me. Because it is a book, its content is relatively permanent and retrievable. I can know beforehand much of what will be said in the church's prayers, and I can look back afterward to see the context of meaning into which my life's moments were set.

The givenness may be thought of as a liturgical expression of the givenness of the gospel. I am not my creator and redeemer. I am not and God is. I am not the measure of the meaning of my own existence. I learn the meaning of my existence as I engage deeply with life under the informing presence of the gospel. And that gospel is a gift. I do not make it; I cannot deal with it honestly if I insist that its good news must meet me on my terms. I do not hold it; it is the power by which I am held. It is the deepest secret of my own existence, yet it is a secret which was spoken to me. I could not have devised or imagined it.

Rather similarly, the *Book of Common Prayer* is mine. I am released and fulfilled, and at times corrected, by it. My life is given meaning, center, hope and purpose through the worship of God which it orders and informs. But the Prayer Book comes to me as something with authority—not with the authority of canon law so much as with the authority of a great expression of a great gospel.

The Prayer Book is made mine through bonds of love and debt. It is mine somewhat as my country is mine or my language is mine. I spend a lifetime, under its unhurried instruction, slowly discovering what it knew all along and what it will tell me when I am ready to hear.

Of course, any liturgy is a human construction. No emphasis on its givenness should suggest that it descended, ready-made from heaven. We are not well informed about the processes by which the first Prayer Books were drafted in the sixteenth century, but we know about the large revision that has been made in our own time. It was a lengthy process involving committees, commissions, staff work, thousands of meetings, reams of paper, drafts and criticisms, revisions, scholarship, vision, pastoral practicality, compromise and political skill. Most generations of Anglicans have received the Prayer Book as it was and left it to their children only slightly altered. It could almost seem a thing outside of history and change. But this generation knows, as few since 1549 could have, that the Prayer Book is made by the church. The great catholic liturgical heritage has been repossessed and refashioned by a church freshly taking responsibility for its own life of worship and prayer. Unmistakably, we make the Prayer Book.

Yet in a profounder sense, the Prayer Book makes us. We are not so much its parents as its grateful children. The very lessons in faith which inform our impulse to change it have been taught by it. It has its own vitality and its own standards of integrity. We do not have complete control over it, for one does not use or manipulate that which one loves. The Prayer Book can only be revised responsibly by those who have first respected it, listened to it and been nurtured by it. We may change it in ways appropriate to its own genius and its own sources; otherwise it had best not be changed at all.

This givenness of the principal vehicle of Anglican liturgy expresses something profound about the very interior of worship. Of course, in one sense, any act of worship is ours. It is we who sing and make eucharist and pray for the world we care about. Only when liturgy is concrete and present can we identify deeply with it. But in a profounder sense, worship is not ours, but is a gift. We do not make it; we receive it. It is the overflowing divine joy reaching into our life and returning through the free response of the creation. It is the age-long voice of dependent, thankful, forgiven, aspiring humanity, sounding freshly in our present. We shall be much too self-important if we suppose that worship starts with us. It has been there all along. Through the Prayer Book we participate in an ongoing hymn of praise.

3. Something taken for granted by regular users of the Prayer Book but remarked at once by persons who come to it without prior familiarity, is the formedness, craftedness, structuredness of its whole and its parts. Prayer Book worship does not have a rambling, associational flow, nor is it static and repetitive. The services have considered shape and design. Things have beginnings, middles and ends. Actions follow one another in intelligible sequence. Time moves by meaningful contrasts of anticipation and arrival, fast and feast. Days, weeks, seasons and years are brought into an expressive, Christocentric shaping of time. The sacramental events stand in significant relation to one another. On every page there is evidence of care for balance of emphasis and for the word or phrase with appropriate weight and nuance.

This pervasive character warrants attention, for, at least since the emergence of the Romantic impulse, form has, in much popular estimate, not been highly regarded, especially in things of the human spirit. Free, unpredictable inner life has seemed self-validating, while form has seemed imposed, alien and alienating. Insofar as I must give attention to formal requirements, I am diverted from listening to the true voice of feeling. But neither life nor art can usefully be analysed in such stark antitheses. Form and feeling need one another. Even that art which cultivates randomness and spontaneity bears witness to the discipline and discrimination that lie behind and give authority to the free gesture. Art that convinces and communicates may conceal form, but does not abandon it.

Any vital, all-at-once imaginative impulse seems to require some ordering, arrangement or sequence. It seeks a form organically connected with its inmost life. The struggle to bring the originating impulse to adequate expression seems to fulfil the impulse itself. Forceful, life-illuminating art is that which unites something worth expressing with a mastery of technique which assures it of full development.

Liturgy is not merely an art form, but it is not less than an art form. Distinctively the voice of Christian prayer rises from the community which responds in faith to God made known in Jesus Christ. But that faith should not have to express itself in superficial, careless, or sentimental prayers, hymns, or liturgical events. In a sense, the interior of the spiritual life of any tradition is validated by the integrity of the external expressions of its public worship.

A worshipper who uses the *Book of Common Prayer* today is a sharer in ancient, basic liturgical structures. In its earliest generations, the Christian community adapted the Jewish forms of the synagogue meeting, the household meal, and the liturgical week and year. Informed by its deep Christological vision, the young church turned these forms into celebrations of the Christian message, signs of the believing community, and ritual enactments of faith. These early, elemental forms have proved remarkably durable. When they have become distorted, someone reasserts their clarity and purpose. Groups which have parted with them tend to rediscover or reinvent them.

The Prayer Book is, of course, no more than one of the situationally-conditioned guises in which these forms have appeared. It has changed and it will change again. It appeals for its own authority to the Bible and the early church. It is a contemporary representation of a life that originated as the Christian movement originated. Through loyalty to the *Book of Common Prayer*, one is made a participant in the great, constitutive liturgical actions to which the Prayer Book itself is loyal.

But these liturgical forms are not significant just because they are very old. They may be considered forms which—with all their variability and adaptability—are somehow bound integrally into the life of faith. Their structure is the structure of the redemptive life. Faith has created these signs and they are still the ways by which faith is known and shared. One need not look far to find other forms which are similarly bonded with the reality they express. Persons in love say to one another, perhaps rather often, "I love you." The sentence is hackneyed. Saying it can become routinized. Yet such a declaration is not readily separated from the reality of which it speaks. Were these words to stop, it would indicate that something had gone wrong in the reality the words should convey. But when love is alive, the thrice-familiar phrase can be alive. Rather similarly, the Prayer Book brings a worshipper into engagement with the realities of faith. Its basic forms have a self-renewing capacity. One only tires of them when one tires of the gospel itself.

The engagement mediated through such benign, generous forms can be an enlargement and a liberation. I come to church with things I want to find and express. But there my expectations meet the firm, genial *Book of Common Prayer*. It welcomes me. It encourages and assists me in saying what I want to say. But it sets my interests alongside others in a large, open movement. It may not have in mind today only what I have in mind. It asks me to say things I had not thought myself especially ready to say. Its balance addresses my one-sidedness. When I am too euphoric, it reminds me of brokenness, of failure, and of the need for confession of sin. When I am in despair, it reminds me of forgiveness greater than sin and hope beyond human destructiveness. It holds before me a realism and a largeness of faith that I seldom have on my own and always need. It reminds me of deep, forgotten things. The Prayer Book reaches into my own experience, kindly, judgingly and redemptively. It does so by setting me within forms which derive from classic apprehensions of the Christian message. I am delivered from the necessity of finding the meaning of my own existence out of my own resources. Those great liturgical forms are mine; I revel in them. Yet they rebuke me, surprise me and extend me. Their very formedness is not oppressive, rather it is a ministry of grace.

4. Another feature of the Prayer Book and the life of prayer which it elicits is its *corporateness*. The Prayer Book speaks throughout in the plural: "we praise you . . . , we confess to you . . . , we give thanks." The Prayer Book is the voice of a praying community, not a manual for private devotions. It is written from and for the collective life.

In worship, the congregation is not like an audience in a darkened hall, listening to five skilled string players, on a lighted stage, doing the Schubert Quintet. In the worshipping assembly of the baptized, there is no audience.

But active, participatory congregational worship is not a simple matter. In complex liturgical action, even though all take part, all do not take the same parts. Some prayers are led by a single person; others are shared between a leader and congregation; others are prayed unitedly. With music and movement, as with words, leadership passes back and forth among a variety of persons. For such an action to go along with economy and simplicity, it is desirable to have a printed text giving design and sequence to the whole—somewhat as those five string players have a musical score which lets each one take his or her part and coordinate it with the others. The score is well-thumbed and penciled, for in rehearsals the players have had to establish their interior sympathy with the music and work out their unified interpretation. But at the concert, discussion is finished; subtle signals among the players are reduced to an unobtrusive minimum; all is transparent; Schubert is in charge.

Corporate worship of the sort the Prayer Book makes possible implies some theological, ecclesiological understandings. Life is communal. Redemption is communal. To be and to be a Christian is to exist in a body of close relationships. The life of faith is not a solitary communion with God. Rather, Christians are set in the midst of interpersonal bondings in which each has much to receive and much to give. There are, to be sure, unshared and unsharable reaches of each person. This inner uniqueness needs appropriate development and expression. In my association with others, I cannot derive what I need nor contribute what I might if I am not working at the exacting and never-ending task of understanding and possessing myself. The whole self, in its shared and its unshared aspects, is open to God. God knows me as no one else knows me and as I do not know myself. But God has set me in communities—some intimate, and some more remote and impersonal—which require of me responsible love. A large part of my communion with and service for God is carried out in these social solidarities. Those are the terms of my existence.

Now there are styles of prayer appropriate to the expression of myself-as-individual and styles suited to the expression of myself-as-member. In my conscious communion with God, I need to give voice to the depth of my own inwardness. In such prayer, I can be as methodical or as unmethodical as I wish. After all, no one else is listening in. I can lose my train of thought and no harm is done. I can try different ways of devotion, searching for what is authentic and rewarding for me. I can put myself under discipline and I can remove myself from it. The one thing I cannot allow myself to be is dilettantist in this serious business of the self's custody of itself. Unless I have a life of private prayer, my participation in corporate prayer will be limited. I will not bring much to it nor derive much from it. But if private prayer is my sole or dominating form of prayer, I shall develop a privatized, self-enclosed spiritual experience. I cannot know or express myself truly apart from the strong bonds which unite me with others. I need the enlargement and corrective of shared confession of collective sin. My compassion needs to be gripped in common intercessions. I need to contribute to, and at times to be carried by, the communal praise. I need the actual, embodied presence of others, and the tangible sacramental actions by which lives are linked to one another in the life of Christ.

Corporate prayer is not just simultaneous private prayers, nor is it one person doing private prayer in public. Truly corporate prayer requires of all participants certain special skills and sensitivities, few of which are acquired automatically. An eloquent, significant, complex but focused action is carried out by a congregation in which all have responsible parts. In complementary ways, leadership passes among persons who act according to competence, training and appointment. The whole is flawed to the extent that it becomes a showpiece for the virtuosity of one or more of the participants or is dominated by a leader who becomes self-consciously dramatic or must exceed his or her assigned role. Liturgical worship (like chamber music playing) calls for modesty among those who carry individual parts, so that the whole can be convincing. Worshippers need to internalize the liturgy and its demands well enough so that they can contribute and be led while at the same time remaining free to concentrate on God and the world rather than on the mechanics of posture, wordings, page turning and musical settings. (There are things to be said in behalf of routinization.) As a Christian, I am a member, and I must acquire the skills for praying as such.

By the character of its content and by the fact that it is officially authorized, the Prayer Book represents the church's prayers. The book in the pew is a sign of the participation of each individual in the prayer of the congregation and of each congregation in the prayer of the great, ecumenical, time-embracing community of faith. Anglicanism has prescribed no official or preferred guides to the cultivation of private devotional skills—as though if that were provided for, corporate worship, as simply the aggregate of private prayer, would take care of itself. Rather, the Anglican way has given priority to what we say together before God. The many styles of private prayer that will develop in the free atmosphere of Anglicanism should be, in some measure, derived from and answerable to the *Book of Common Prayer*. The church can have a just role in shaping the church's prayers; it has no comparable responsibility or competence in directing the private prayer of each member. Yet by setting forth a rich, generous liturgy for corporate worship, all private or group prayer will be given an inspiration and a standard. And each church member will have been introduced to the joy and task of the special sort of prayer with which all begins and beyond which one never moves—the joy and task of learning to pray with the church.

5. The Prayer Book is effective in its role as a spacious, perennially fresh shaper of public prayer in great measure because of the *economy* of its style. It concentrates on essentials. It uses short, sayable, breathable sentences, rather than sustained grammatical units. Adjective and adverbs are used sparingly.

This characteristic of the Prayer Book, like many of the others already spoken of, may owe something to the print medium. In an oral/aural culture, bards (and their auditors too, for that matter) can keep in mind hundreds of lines of poetry. People know by tradition the formulaic speech that is required for ceremonial occasions, religious or social. But once print has entered a culture, the knack of doing these formal things spontaneously tends to break down. Free oral expression tends to become diffuse, discursive, repetitive and to ride loose to grammar. Careful expression comes to mean prepared, written expression which, of course, may then be read or recited.

One can observe that when clergy depart from the Prayer Book, they usually add words. Unless such interpolations are made sparingly and sensitively, a discriminating worshipper has the feeling that the simplicity and directness of the Prayer Book is being subverted by clerical fanciness, folksiness or pretentiousness. Without wanting to compare one's own tradition with one less familiar nor to minimize the better moments in extempore worship, one can perhaps fairly say that worship which makes no use of prepared and printed texts takes on the less desirable characteristics of conversational speech—an associational, random flow, with an excess of words, a reliance on ready-to-hand stock phrases and thinness of content. Probably most persons familiar with the Prayer Book have a sense that much significance is compressed into individual sentences, collect-length prayers, or entire offices. In an hour or so of worship, a great deal happens. And because so much is there for one, the words can be returned to over and over with a grateful feeling that they have more to impart.

This less-is-more characteristic of the Prayer Book is in part a matter of rhetoric. The sixteenth century compilers, with the Medieval service books as their sources, carried over the compressed style of liturgical Latin into strong English. But the characteristic also stems from a sense of what liturgy should talk about. The Prayer Book was drafted in an argumentative time, but it does not argue. (The earliest Prayer Books contained some direct efforts to educate. But their "exhortations" have not worn well and have been progressively eliminated, either in church practice or in the revisions of the text itself.) The Prayer Book does not have towering periods of rhetoric meant to elicit or compel our feelings. Rather, it is dominated by rich affirmations of the character and ways of God. God's grace is there before we think to draw on it. Our love is response to God's prior love for us. Our future is secured finally in divine promise. Over and over, the Prayer Book sets our confused human life within the adequacy of God.

The Prayer Book's characteristic, single-minded reference of everything to God means it is strong at a place where most contemporary awareness is weak, and it is rather summary just where we have a great deal to say. We live in an age which is obsessed with self-analysis and not very confident about God. When we compose new prayers or paraphrase old ones, we tend to psychologize. We explore our states of consciousness, or we linger over the ambiguities of things. But we are not very good at setting such material in a framework of theological affirmation.

The modern faith community seems to call, from deep within itself, for experiments which use new liturgical forms and styles appropriate to unprecedented new experience. So we create occasions in which we can, as it were, hold up before ourselves and before God the urgent things that are taking place outside us and inside us. The *American Prayer Book 1979* (like most other modern liturgies) invites such creativity within its structures. The liturgical tradition, reaching us as it does from past ages and speaking as it does in a general, public voice, is richer for the particularity and presentism of prayers, litanies and songs from and for today's occasions.

At their best, creative liturgies of today can produce moments of vitality and eloquence—moments eminently contemporary, yet compatible with the fabric of the Prayer Book and the liturgical tradition. But it is hardly cruel to observe that such moments are not frequent. The objectivity and restraint of the Prayer Book elude us today. We turn inward, deploring our self-deceptions and lamenting our doubt and confusion. We use the forms of prayer to preach, often accusing ourselves or promoting a favored cause. Alas, one sometimes encounters oppressive liturgies about liberation or heavy liturgies about celebration.

But whether at their best or at less than their best, modern liturgies do not seem very enduring. Perhaps they should not be expected to be. If they articulate a moment in the life of faith (or faith and doubt) today, that is not to be despised. Yet profound prayer does not simply express its situation, but interprets it. The contemporary prayers most commonly encountered betray their captivity to a moment in time and a location in the social order. Even when they speak energetically and sensitively, they tend to tell us what we already know.

Such prayer, for its own sake, needs to be held within the theistic structures of the liturgical tradition. The *Book of Common Prayer* has one immensely rich thing to say, and an idiom appropriate for saying it. The Prayer Book is convinced that the ends of human existence lie in God and that only God can enable us to know, trust, love, worship and serve God. It therefore prays that the God to whom all hearts are open, who knows all desires, and from whom no secrets are hidden, will cleanse the thoughts of our hearts by the in-breathing of the Spirit. What God expects, God alone can give. There is in the Prayer Book a great deal of the self-knowledge we seek urgently today. But it is presented in a reality scheme in which it is taken for granted that we can only understand or deal with our own condition when we bring our helplessness into relation to the strong love of God.

The foregoing points have not so much described features of the Prayer Book as they have examined an interaction between the Prayer Book and the contemporary worshipper. Some modern literary criticism has found it useful to interpret stories or poems as verbal actions which are in dialogue with their readers. Any literary work with a strongly marked character requires something of us and does something to us. It is much the same with any good liturgical text. Perhaps we have here one of the deep reasons for the uneasiness over Prayer Book revision. What is changing is not just a book but a relation between a book and a people. When the Prayer Book changes, our attitudes towards it and our ways of using it need, in some measure, to be reconsidered and relearned. We are changing the thing that, in the long run, will change us, and we do not know in advance what the new book will give to us or require of us.

Since the Prayer Book comes to us in part from outside our own time, it contains, in form and substance, assumptions that would not inevitably be suggested by our twentieth-century experience. To a certain extent the Prayer Book can seem a witness against the spirit of the age, but just because it transcends the provincial blind spots of our time, it can speak in our time judgingly and redemptively. Its very strangeness can open new possibility, but its deepest secrets are opened on its terms, not on ours. When we consent to it, liturgical worship yields profound inner rewards. The spacious formedness of the Prayer Book, for all its apparent fixity, is full of surprise. There is still, as there has been in the past, sustained interest and delight for Christians who are engaged with this benign tutor in prayer.

VII

Music as an Expression of Anglican Spirituality

Alastair Cassels-Brown

At first glance, the link between music and Anglican spirituality may not be obvious. Yet it is this simple: Anglican spirituality is rooted in the Church's liturgical life.[1] Liturgical music serves two purposes; it is an offering of praise in the context of the liturgy and it enhances the liturgy.[2]

The music of the Anglican Church is as varied in style as the ceremonial. As the ceremonial varies from simple to elaborate, the music varies from simple congregational settings for use in parishes to elaborate choral anthems for use in Cathedrals. Since the Tractarian movement in the last century, these have overlapped.

Because the field is large, the music selected for discussion will be mostly limited to congregational settings which are peculiarly Anglican or which were nurtured in the Anglican tradition. No comparison is made with the music of other communions.

Anglican Chant

Anglican chant is unique. It grew out of traditions that go back to pre-Christian times; notably, Hebrew cantillation gave us form and tunes, influencing Gregorian chant, which in turn provided a form for Anglican chant.[3]

Chant was the answer to setting prose to music. Unlike hymns, which have some form of poetical metre, prose by definition consists of lines containing unequal numbers of syllables. Even Hebrew poetry, which was based on a set number of feet, contained a varying number of syllables within the feet, and consequently, the line. In Gregorian, (called plain song, cantus planus, on plainchant interchangably), any number of syllables can be accommodated by the chant. A few syllables at the end of the line are assigned to the chant melody, the other syllables are sung to a monotone (one note) called a reciting tone.

121

Ex. 1

Hymnal, 1940: #603, v. 1
used by permission

Anglican Chant developed from harmonizations built around chant tones.

Ex. 2

Hymnal, 1940: #603, v. 1
used by permission

Despite its name, Anglican chant was not necessarily an English invention. The following example is by a Flemish composer.

Ex. 3

Oxford Companion to Music
2nd edition 1943
Oxford University Press

The form failed to develop on the continent, probably due to the popularity of the Metrical Psalm. In England, prose versions of the psalms continued to be used concurrently with metrical psalms.

From the foregoing, Anglican chant can be defined as a harmonized melody adapted to the singing of prose. It consists generally of seven trochaic feet with a caesura after the third foot. Often it occurs in duple, and less often in triple and quadruple form.[4]

In common with plain chant, the music is a vehicle for the words; the words are primary, the music is secondary. From this derives an important aspect of performance; the rhythm of chant is the rhythm of deliberate speech. In the past, and even today, there has been a tendency to gabble the words on the reciting tone and to slow up at the cadence (ending); this is an aspect of what became known as Anglican thump. This gabbling denies the primacy of the words and falsely asserts the primacy of the music, with dire results. The cure is simply and effectively prescribed in the *Hymnal, 1940*: to say the words deliberately, to monotone the words in the same rhythm, and lastly, to sing the words to the chant in the same rhythm. Everyone starts by taking a breath together, and everyone keeps together by keeping the all important accented syllables together.[5]

Until about 1860, cathedrals and parish churches did their own pointing, i.e. inserted marks in the text to indicate which words went with which notes of the chant. Since that time, many printed versions have appeared, notably *The Cathedral Psalter*, (edited by Stainer and others), *The Oxford Psalter*, (edited by Lee, Roper and Stewart), *The Parish Psalter*, (edited by Nicholson), and *The American Oxford Psalter*, (edited by Brown).[6]

Since spirituality is much concerned with practical things, we will examine pointing from two opposing positions—that of leaving the change till late in the line and that of making the change early in the line.

The first school points out the historical aspect of Anglican chant. It was originally harmonization of plain chant. Like plain chant, the reciting tone must be left as late as possible. Like plain chant, the last note of the chant must be matched to one syllable only.

Ex. 4

(Hymnal, #680: v. 3b)

The second school argues that primary accents in the words need to be matched to primary accents in the music. This often results in the early leaving of the reciting tone. Also, this often results in clusters of syllables to individual notes in the chant, including the last note.

Ex. 5

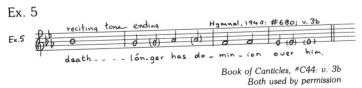

Book of Canticles, #C44: v. 3b
Both used by permission

Both schools maintain that their settings are easiest to sing, though the second appears to be more complicated. In the second model, the emphasis on the last note of the chant is an example of Anglican thump, because of the extra emphasis of more than one syllable.

Both models have weaknesses. The plain chant model is inadequate for English prose, since more than half the endings of lines end in accented syllables. By contrast, there is not one strong ending in the Latin Psalter. In certain cases, to avoid singing more than one syllable to the final note of the chant, one syllable will be slurred over two notes. Another issue is that Anglican chants contain upward leaps implying accents that are not present in Gregorian chants.

The weakness in the primary accents model is that too much is implied from inaccurate musical notation. Half-notes are traditional: in the sixteenth century they indicated short duration. The bar lines are a subsequent accretion.[7] Since the rhythm of speech approximates 189 syllables to the minute, the notes in a chant are better represented by eighth notes.

Ex. 6

In ex. 6b, the only primary accent now remaining is on the reciting tone. The other primary accents have become secondary. The primary accents model is founded on a fallacy.

The chant settings in *The Hymnal, 1940* were an attempt at compromise, which we like to think is a strength of the Anglican Church.

Ex. 7 a. And a great King/above all Gods. (Hymnal, #612: v. 3b)

7 b. And a great/King above all Gods. (Hymnal, #610: v. 3b)

(The first example is the plain chant setting, the second is the Anglican chant setting. The plain chant setting leaves the reciting tone later than the Anglican setting.)

Ex. 8

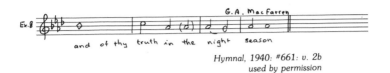

and of thy truth in the night season

Hymnal, 1940: #661: v. 2b
used by permission

This example shows two syllables on the final note. The word *night* is slurred over two notes. However, taken as a whole, *The Hymnal, 1940* leans toward the plain chant model.

The next official book of settings was *Song for Liturgy*, published in 1971. This was also a compromise, which leaned gently to the primary accents mode. *The Book of Canticles* followed in 1979, based on the primary accents model. A comparison of examples nos. 4 and 5 show the uncompromising approach.

While the above examples are all taken from Episcopal sources, they can be matched with similar examples of settings from England. All versions can sound lovely if properly sung.

A story is told of the great composer, Antonin Dvorak, hearing Anglican chant sung in St. Paul's Cathedral, London. "It is beautiful," he is said to have remarked, "but why do they keep singing that silly little tune over and over again?" Not being familiar with the language, he missed the point of chant. He ought to have been listening to the words. What then is the purpose of the music?

At a practical level, the music helps a congregation keep together. At a higher level, it offers opportunity for people to raise their voices together, in sisterhood and brotherhood. (The best kind of singing generates a sense of campfire warmth.) At a higher level still, music enhances the words of canticles and psalms. At its highest level, chant has an almost hypnotic power to raise people's spirits to a new level—poetical or mystical—because its wings carry us up into timelessness. In chanting, this timelessness is perhaps derived from the mantra effect of the repetition of the music, combined with the rhythm of the words, and the dying away in volume at the mediation and the final ending of the line.

Anglican Hymnody

Like the hymnody of other branches of Christianity, the hymnody of the Anglican Church is eclectic, being drawn from many different times and countries.

The Anglican contribution to hymnody since the Reformation includes poems by Joseph Addison, Phineas Fletcher, William Cowper, Christopher Smart, George Herbert, Lord Alfred Tennyson, Charles Wesley, (who said of himself, "I have lived, and I die in the Communion of the Church of England."),[8] Charles Kingsley, Rudyard Kipling, John Masefield and Christina Rossetti; it includes tunes by Thomas Tallis, Orlando Gibbons, Thomas Campian, Jeremiah Clark, William Croft, Thomas Arne, Henry Purcell, Gustav Holst, Leo Sowerby and Ralph Vaughan Williams. These are poets whose works are found in *The Oxford Book of English Verse* or composers whose works are performed in concerts.

In a survey conducted by the Episcopal Church's Standing Commission on Church Music, completed in the first quarter of 1979, hymn words and tunes were listed separately by the number of positive votes for retention. In the top ten texts, only one of the above poets was listed, Charles Wesley, who is listed two and a quarter times—the quarter being the last verse added to the Tate and Brady hymn, "Jesus Christ is risen today." In the top ten tunes, not one of the above composers is listed. The tune, *Sine Nomine*, ("For all the saints") by Vaughan Williams placed 33rd, narrowly beating *Three Kings of Orient* ("We three Kings of Orient are"), placed 36th, which in turn beat Tallis's Canon ("Glory to thee, my God, this night"). In the circumstances, it is with something of a sigh of relief that one fails to find any of the poets or composers listed above represented in the bottom ten. Who was involved in this survey? "Liturgical leaders," parish clergy and music directors of some 7,500 parishes, of whom more than 2,200 replied.[9]

If the results of the survey are useful as a guide to the Anglican Church as a whole, it is evident that eclecticism means more than pure Anglicanism, for there are four non-Anglican derived texts and seven non-Anglican derived tunes in the top ten. By concert hall standards, only one of those tunes is by a great composer, Mendelssohn; the tune, "Hark, the Herald Angels sing," was described by the composer as unsuitable for sacred words.[10]

Five of the top ten tunes are folksong or simple chant. Folksong has long been a popular element in hymnody. The implication is profound. Bela Bartok, who collected over 2,000 folk tunes, said:
"I am convinced that any one of our melodies that derive from the 'folk' in the strict sense of the word is an archetype of artistic perfection at its highest standard. I regard them as masterpieces in miniature, just as I regard a Bach fugue or a Mozart sonata."[11]
If Bartok is right, the smallest parish can sing the finest music in the world. The survey showed that the folk songs included in supplement II were popular, for five folk tunes and one metrical psalm tune were rated in the top ten tunes for that booklet. (Supplements III and IV are too new to have been evaluated by the survey.) The most significant feature of hymnody in the twentieth century may well be the revival of folk song.

The survey indirectly gives us the relative popularity of hymns from different periods. In the first hundred, five are plain-song; seven are traditional; fourteen are from the sixteenth century (including four metrical psalm tunes); fourteen are from the seventeenth century (including nine German Chorales); twenty-three from the eighteenth century; thirty from the nineteenth century; seven from the twentieth century. Taking all 600 hymns, the last ten include five from the last half of the nineteenth century. If there are surprises in these figures, one surprise is that the hymns from the last half of the nineteenth century, which constitute about a third of all the hymns in the hymnal, only rate twenty in the first hundred.

Hymnals

While there is not space here to catalog the output of hymnals, the interest and energy that went into their publication indicates their importance. For instance, nineteen hymnals were published in Britain before 1700; some were promptly suppressed or commercially unsuccessful such as Coverdale's *Goostly Psalms* (1539) or George Wither's book of hymns (1623); others were successful, one going through 600 editions (Sternhold and Hopkins, published by Day, 1561). In the United States, five hymnals were published before 1800, including the *Bay Psalm Book* (1640) which went through seventy editions. Many tune books followed.[12]

After the nonconformist minister, Isaac Watts, had made "human" hymns acceptable, tunes lost their sturdy four-square character. *Lyra Davidica*, published in London, in 1708, contained *Easter Hymn*, a flowing carol tune, familiar to us as "Jesus Christ is risen today." Other flowing tunes followed, like *Rockingham, The First Nowell,* and *Duke Street.*

The first eclectic hymnal was published in 1737 by John and Charles Wesley; it drew on translations from the Greek, from German expressions of Moravian thought, and from Watts, Herbert and others. In 1861, the first edition of *Hymns Ancient and Modern* appeared, subsequently going through many editions and selling millions of copies. Two notable hymnals followed—the *English Hymnal* (1906) which included a large number of plain song melodies in addition to folk melodies and *Songs of Praise* (1925) compiled by its editors Percy Dearmer, Ralph Vaughan Williams and Martin Shaw. New supplements have appeared in the last ten years.

In England, any Anglican Church can use whatever hymnal it chooses. In the United States, the Episcopal Church has only one authorized hymnal in the interests of uniformity, *The Hymnal, 1940* and its supplements. When the new hymnal, presently being prepared, is available, it will be the only authorized hymnal. The texts are being carefully checked for sixteen defects ranging from poor theology to racist and sexist language. Proportionately more folk songs will be included. It will draw on the better hymns from other hymnals. It will introduce hymns that are new. Being the only authorized hymnal means that it must be the best for this time, or it will be disregarded. The *Hymnal, 1940* was excellent as the new supplements indicate; the new hymnal shows promise of being even better.

Since modern Anglicans are not famed for their strong hymn singing, we may wonder why there was so much energy put into publishing hymnals. It was not always so. In the seventeenth and eighteenth centuries, Anglican singing made up in noise for what it lacked in delicacy. "Thomas Mace found it 'sad to hear what whining, toting, yelling, or screeking there is in many congregations.' . . . But some of the clergy, such as John Patrick, Master of the Charterhouse, realized that this 'common way' filled an important role in the worship of the people and resisted the efforts of well-meaning reformers to get rid of it."[13]

All the creative energy, all the hard work, indicate a deep concern for a part of the liturgy that is able to inspire, nurture and bring together the individuals in a congregation: Hilary of Poitiers and Gregory of Nazianzus wrote hymns because they realized the effectiveness of the hymns sustaining the Arians,[14] and Luther said that if he could write the hymns, others might teach the people what they want. At a higher level, there is the warm empathy of enjoying singing together, which is a manifestation of love. At a higher level still, a vision can come to us through the music, in which music becomes an unofficial sacrament of the church, the outward and audible sign of an inward and spiritual grace.

Merbecke, Cranmer and Committees

At the time of the *Prayer Book of 1549*, Cranmer and his ecclesiastical advisers made a far reaching musical pronouncement; John Merbecke was commissioned to set the sung parts of the service with one note to a syllable.[15] The result is musical settings of the greatest clarity and simplicity; it also resulted in a loss of beauty. As an illustration, Winfred Douglas recalled a Bishop on the committee for the *Hymnal, 1940*, who wanted to take out the triplets from *Ton-y-botel*.[16]

Ex. 9

Hymnal, 1940: #519
used by permission

The familiar VIII tone Festival setting of the Magnificat was simplified by Merbecke:

Ex. 10

John Marbeck,
"The Book of Common Prayer"
noted: 1550

Similarly, the Sanctus and Agnus Dei for "when there is a burial" were simplified from the Requiem. Some parts such as the Gloria were newly composed.[17]

The principle of one note to a syllable came to affect Cathedral choral settings; it has become a feature of Anglican music.

Ex. 11

Tudor Church Music
Vol. 4: Oxford University Press

The imposition of limitations in Art can have paradoxical effects: "In limitation is the master made manifest."[18] The hymn tunes of Orlando Gibbons are satisfying, yet the effect is achieved with the simplest of means. Henry Purcell's vigorous and exuberant anthem, "Rejoice in the Lord, Alway," employs one note to a syllable throughout. Simplicity is part of the Anglican ethos.

Cranmer and his advisers were reacting to the kind of abuses mentioned by Erasmus, "Modern church music is so composed that the congregation cannot understand a word."[19] Nearing our own day, the Archbishop's Committee on Music in Worship issued a report in 1922, which emphasized the difference between the Parish situation where the congregation sang all the service, and the cathedral situation where the choir sings everything alone except the hymns. It recommended that the choir be behind the congregation and that the old village orchestras be reinstated in the West gallery to accompany the hymns. Again, one senses that they were reacting to abuses—the copying of the cathedral model by churches lacking the resources or leadership and the congregation being deprived of singing their part of the service. Moving the choir to the West end takes it from the centre of the action. At the same time, the leadership is more effective musically. Using a village orchestra saves installing a gallery organ; it also involves more people as instrumentalists.

In 1951, the same committee's report on *Music in Church* stressed the idea of "nobility" and "dignity" in liturgical music. Eric Routley comments, "There are other qualities . . . contemplativeness, cheerfulness, and integrity."[20] (It had remarkably little effect, for not long after, Beaumont's *XX Century Mass* and the hymns of the XX Century Folk Group spread with astonishing speed on both sides of the Atlantic.

In the Episcopal Church, the Joint Commission on Music, appointed by the General Convention of 1919, produced a report that was adopted by the next convention of 1922. The aim of this report was to achieve "unity of ideals rather than the standardization of methods." Among the recommendations of the report are the preparation and publication (without expense to General Convention) of a congregational service book, a psalter pointed for Anglican chants, and a revised edition of the choral service. Further, it made recommendations for disseminating lists of anthems, services and standard works on church music, through diocesan and provincial conferences.

In 1956, Seabury Press printed *Ideals in Church Music*, an official statement prepared for the Joint Commission on Church Music by Leo Sowerby. The opening presents ideas about the relationship of music to liturgy; it postulates two necessary standards, bringing devotion to the devout, and a satisfying and uplifting experience to the music; after a historical survey of church music, it closes with an appeal for turning our backs on music that is sensuous and pseudoromantic. Regarding the "two necessary standards," it's likely that C. S. Lewis was more realistic when he said that the musically trained ought charitably to accept coarse fare for the sake of bringing others to God, while the unmusical ought charitably to accept what they do not understand as a defect in their own understanding.[21] Yet, Sowerby knew that tastes differ and that we cannot always turn our backs on sensuous and pseudoromantic music; he was postulating an ideal.

Nearly forty years after their first report, the Joint Commission considered that the first report needed revision. Many of its recommendations had been carried out, for instance, the development of the musical edition of the *Hymnal, 1940*, and the development of instruction in church music in our seminaries. After emphasizing the dual purpose of church music—enhancement of the liturgy and offering to God—it quoted Sir Henry Hadow as to three chronic "ills," which are "sentimentalism, theatricalism and virtuosity." It notes the improved congregational participation in the liturgy, further emphasizes the secondary relationship that music bears to the liturgy, contains a consideration of various questions in regard to the *Hymnal* ("Why did you lower the pitch of the tunes?" When does one sing 'Amen'?"), a listing of the sung parts of the service for a priest or congregation, a discussion of the music of the Offices, advice on organs, organists, and choirs, and a concluding note on church schools and collegiate chapels. Although in some instances the Commission is reacting to abuses, such as the installation of electronic organs, this report seems generally more optimistic of high standards being achieved and maintained.

The careful work of committees, the concern that they have lavished that abuses be redressed, the insistence on standards worthy of the worship of Almighty God all point to the importance of music's contribution to the spirituality of the worship offered by the church. This is beautifully expressed in the collect for church musicians and artists, on page 819 of the new prayer book:

"O God, whom saints and angels delight to worship in heaven be ever present with your servants who seek through art and music to perfect the praises offered by your people on earth; and grant to them even now glimpses of your beauty, and make them worthy at length to behold it unveiled for evermore; through Jesus Christ our Lord. Amen."

Footnotes

1 Harvey H. Guthrie, *see above*, chapter 1.

2 Leo Sowerby, *Ideals in Church Music* (Greenwich, Connecticut: Seabury, 1956), p. 5; see also, the Joint Commission on Church Music *Report to General Convention*, (New York: H. W. Gray, 1961).

3 Willi Apel, *Gregorian Chant* (Bloomington: Indiana University Press, 1958), pp. 34-35.

4 Percy A. Scholes, *The Oxford Companion to Music* (London: Oxford University Press, 1970), pp. 32, 34.

5 In *The Hymnal of the Protestant Episcopal Church*, 1940. (New York: Church Pension Fund), pp. 697ff.

6 Scholes, Ibid., p. 35.

7 Mary Fenwick, *Anglican Chant, Music*, August, 1977, pp. 32ff.

8 John Julian, *A Dictionary of Hymnology*, Vol. II, (New York: Dover, 1957), p. 1258.

9 Diocesan Press Service of the Episcopal Church, *Church Music Survey Completed* (New York: The Communication Office of the Episcopal Church Centre, April 1979).

10 In *The Hymnal 1940 Companion*, (New York: The Church Pension Fund, 1951), p. 22.

11 Quoted by Roman Ryterbrand, no source given, *The Folk Harp Journal*, June 1976.

12 Scholes, Ibid., pp. 506-7.

13 The Old Way of Singing, *The Musical Times*, November 1979, p. 943.

14 Winfred Douglas, *Church Music in History and Practice* (New York: Charles Scribner's Sons, 1962), p. 131.

15 Ibid., p. 56.

16 Ibid., p. 67.

17 John Merbecke, *The Book of Common Praier Noted* (London: Richard Grafton, 1550).

18 Goethe, *Natur und Kunst*, in Julius Geobel, *Goethe's Poems* (New York: Henry Holt, 1901), p. 136.

19 Owen Chadwick, *The Reformation* (Great Britain: Pelican, 1972), p. 436.

20 Eric Routley, *Church Music and the Christian Faith* (Carol Stream, Illinois: Agape, c. 1978), p. 82.

21 C. S. Lewis, *On Church Music:* in W. Hooper, ed. C. S. Lewis: *Christian Reflections* (Grand Rapids: Erdmans, 1967) pp. 96-97.

VIII

An Incarnational Spirituality

John E. Skinner

Process philosophy, as this has been identified particularly with
the thought of Alfred North Whitehead, has been influencing
theological understanding slowly during the past several decades.
The philosophy itself is so difficult to learn because of the peculiar
style of Whitehead that only in the recent past has there been any
attempt to translate these philosophical subtleties into more
obvious theological and philosophical meanings. Anglican
thinkers, such as William Temple, Lionel Thornton, and later,
Norman Pittenger, have found Whitehead's philosophy useful in
exploring theological themes. In fact, the incarnational emphasis
of Anglicanism has been complemented by the dynamic categories of process philosophy.

Process philosophy today is in a position similar to that of
Aristotle in the thirteenth century. This strange Hellenic philosophy
which was so difficult to understand, after many years of intellectual and spiritual struggle and discipline, became the philosophical foundation for the *Summa* of St. Thomas Aquinas.
Aristotle was a corrective in that time to some of the exaggerations
of various kinds of Platonism and their influence on theological inquiry.

The philosophical views of Whitehead are supported by developments in other areas of human inquiry. His philosophy of nature
or cosmology is an attempt to make sense out of the revolution in
physics which took place in the latter part of the nineteenth and
the early part of the twentieth century. Advances in human
understanding based on evolutionary theories are also an important part of the intellectual situation which is contemporary with
Whitehead's point of view. The philosophy of Henri Bergson as
well as the work done by C. Lloyd Morgan, Samuel Alexander,
and Jan Christiaan Smuts, present a dynamic view of nature and
human being based on theories of emergent evolution. Of course,
the person known best in this area among theologians today is
Pierre Teilhard de Chardin, the distinguished paleontologist and

Jesuit priest. An important supporter of these attempts to construct philosophies of nature was the Anglican scholar, Canon
Charles Raven.

Anglicanism has always expressed an incarnational perspective
in theology. Whitehead, although not a theologian, was the son
of an Anglican priest and nurtured in that religious ethos. In a
careful study of his work it is possible to ascertain that one of his
fundamental themes is that of St. John's Gospel, the Word was
made flesh. One might say that his cosmology is a secularized
version in current scientific and philosophical understanding of
that Johannine insight.

Many years ago Martin Thornton in his book *Christian
Proficiency* developed an account of prayer and spirituality based
on the Neo-Thomism of Eric Mascall. This book was very influential in certain sectors of Anglicanism and in other parts of Christendom as well. Recently Thornton found that the philosophical
underpinnings for this book were inadequate. Aristotle and his
concepts of nature, human beings and God do not do justice to
the many new insights uncovered. As a result, Thornton wrote
another book, *Prayer: A New Encounter*, in which he used John
Macquarrie's *Principles of Christian Theology* as a foundation.
Macquarrie's perspective is existentialist. Christian theology is
articulated within that kind of understanding. The result: A much
more dynamic approach to prayer and spirituality.

One of the difficulties, however, with using existentialism,
particularly the type derived from the thought of Martin
Heidegger, is that it has a deficiency in its concept of nature.
Nature is viewed primarily as an alien, static, wholly objectified
kind of reality which the human being to some extent must resist
in order to find true authenticity as a person or self. The static
views of nature characteristic of the teachings of Descartes and
Newton still hover in the background.

It is here that the need for a more dynamic approach to nature
is dramatized. It is more in line with the important affirmations of
the existentialists that such a dynamic outlook be developed.
Consequently, many theologians have found that existential
teachings about human beings are complemented by a process
view of nature which results in the emergence from nature of a
dynamic, human person. Whitehead and some of the existentialists
may thus converge.

It is my contention that the existential contributions to a theology of prayer and spirituality made by Martin Thornton, John Macquarrie and others can be enriched and aided by the articulation of what might be called, an incarnational spirituality. And such an incarnational spirituality expressed in dynamic process terms can serve well both Anglican theological inquiry and spiritual discipline.

Spirit: Its Various Meanings

In common usage the word, spirit, has many meanings. Perhaps the most basic is related to wind or breath, in the Old Testament *ruach* and in the New Testament *pneuma*. It is often understood as the breath of life and therefore an animating force or principle. Related to this is the word inspire or inspiration which is derived from the Latin word, *spirare*, which means to breathe or to blow. In this connection spirit is akin to life and is in contrast to non-life. When non-life or inorganic categories tend to dominate the understanding, often spirit is something dissociated from matter, or from body, and becomes a kind of free-floating phenomenon or even apparition. Here "spirits" are seen as divine or demonic and they are considered to be influential in determining the fate of humankind.

The word is also used in a number of other ways. In some instances it refers to the characteristics of mind or temperament in a person, a free or courageous spirit. Moreover, it may describe enthusiastic loyalty as in school spirit; or it may be a word denoting the spirit of a group (*esprit de corps*), a kind of universal self, the cohesive force uniting the group; what sociologists call "the social self" of a group or political structure. In addition, it may reflect a disposition or mental attitude, such as being in good spirits today. In the area of literary and Biblical interpretation, it can have reference to the real meaning of a passage rather than a distortion caused by abstracting the passage from its context and then emphasizing the dead letter (letter vs. spirit).

In contrast to these meanings of spirit, some of its antonyms are apathetic, lethargic, stolid, passive and conformal. The antonyms of spirit demonstrate that in the basic meaning of the word, initiative, free expression, adventure and risk are characteristic of the spirited being. This implies a dynamic rather than a static emphasis.

This contrast was illustrated dramatically for me when a friend introduced me to his Dalmatian. My experience with Dalmatians has been one in which a highly imaginative, often unpredictable, always delightful, usually playful canine confronts one with a zest and adventure not found among many other breeds. Some people find that this expression of spirit is distasteful in an animal, but a Dalmatian is that kind of remarkable canine anomaly. My friend, however, overtrained his dog and the result was a lethargic, passive, sad and frustrated canine. The poor animal was only a semblance of the dog he should have been. Conformal obedience took precedence over that delicate balance between necessary obedience and living spirit. When it was my pleasure and privilege to share obedience training with my Dalmatian, my dog and I agreed that we would not take it with ultimate seriousness. Instead, we became co-conspirators against transforming a vibrant canine organism into a perfectly behaved spotted mechanism.

Dualism: Body and Soul; Flesh and Spirit

Western Civilization has been haunted by a persistent dualism between body and soul, flesh and spirit, matter and mind. If body, flesh and matter are understood primarily as static substances, then soul, mind or spirit becomes a kind of animating reality. The history of this dualism is presented by D. R. G. Owen in his study *Body and Soul*. Owen draws a distinction between what he calls a religious point of view derived from Greek religious practices, particularly the Orphics, and the Biblical perspective of Jews and Christians. The familiar dualism is more characteristic of the so-called religious outlook while Biblical emphases tend in the direction of a psychosomatic wholeness in human beings. Some dualism may be found in Biblical sources, but Owen concludes that this is due precisely to the influence of these religious emphases on Biblical writers during the Exile and beyond.

The most apparent dualism in the New Testament has been cited in St. Paul's contrast between flesh and spirit. Popularly, this contrast has been interpreted as my human flesh in conflict with my human spirit. In this case the soul or spirit is imprisoned in its bodily or fleshly jail and needs liberation by some kind of spiritual salvation. This dualism in St. Paul is only an apparent one, if Owen and also J. A. T. Robinson in his monograph *The Body* are correct. St. Paul is actually speaking about two solidarities or corporate involvements. According to the flesh means a solidarity with all other human beings in Adam, in alienation from God, and also in estrangement from one another. Flesh is thus a term denoting an alienated humanity. According to the spirit, on the other hand, means being in Christ. This involves liberation from the old solidarity in Adam and a participation in a solidarity of reconciliation with God, nature and one's fellow human beings. Spirit in this usage means a new creation, or what Paul Tillich called, a new being.

In the seventeenth century this dualism of body and soul was firmly ensconced in our philosophical and scientific traditions by René Descartes. Descartes reduced reality to two fundamental substances totally isolated from one another. One substance was extension (*res extensa*) and the other was thought (*res cogitans*).

The extended thing or substance was what became the quantified nature of the seventeenth and eighteenth centuries. All qualitative aspects (value, life, mental and other components) were exorcised by Descartes in this mathematically quantified materiality.

The other substance was thought, or the thinking thing. This wholly mental or conceptual reality, mind or soul, was totally isolated and alienated from the quantified natural necessity of matter or the extended thing. This isolated soul or thought, moreover, was alienated from other souls or thoughts. This teaching was articulated later by Leibniz when he developed a concept of monads without windows. By this he meant substances which were incapable of entering into an intersubjective or interpersonal relationship with one another. The only way in which body and soul or matter and mind could be coordinated in the Cartesian position was through the intervention of a *deus ex machina*, a God conveniently posited in order to solve difficulties caused by exclusion and neglect in this kind of dualism.

The dualism of Descartes has served well the model of nature as mechanism proposed by Newton, and it has occasioned a spiritual antagonism that is still with us. When human life and being are reduced to behavioristic explanations as found in the psychology of B. F. Skinner and others, soul and spirit are lost in a mechanistic reduction. The necessary reaction to this deformity is an alienated spirituality which wishes to cut itself loose from such dangerous distortions and neglects.

Descartes was unable to account for life or the organic realm in his philosophy, and so all nonhuman life was categorized in a

mechanistic manner. Since mechanism or extended things have
no feeling, then all nonhuman life is without feeling, without sensitivity. So from this point of view my Dalmatian was nothing but a
very complicated natural machine with no feeling, no emotion, no
spirit. In fact it also follows that such an animal does not feel pain
when hurt because machines feel no pain or discomfort; they only
malfunction at times.

Needless to say, such a conclusion is absurd. But this dissociation of sensibility, to use T. S. Eliot's phrase, has unfortunately
not only influenced our attitudes towards animals, but also has
tended to become more prominent than we would like to think in
the way we treat one another as human beings.

In the twentieth century, a noted Oxford philosopher, Gilbert
Ryle, was able to dispatch the ghost (soul) from the machine, in
his book *The Concept of Mind*. Although it was not his intention,
what we end up with is the machine only. The human person, as
a result, takes his or her place among the many natural or fabricated machines and the reductionism is complete. The dualism is
defeated through the destruction of vibrant soul or spirit.

Spirit As Fundamental Contrast

Although Descartes and his followers prevailed in the early
modern centuries, voices of protest to such distortions were raised
often. Blaise Pascal was adamant in his refusal to accept the spiritually destructive implications of such thought. His famous statement about the heart which has its reasons which reason does not
know was a way of declaring that a vast area of experience,
human and nonhuman, was being neglected. He posited instead
a fundamental contrast in human existence as expressing more
fully human life and experience.

Pascal saw the human person as an expression of both angel
and beast. He visualized the human being as hovering within the
midst of these two exaggerated limits, a little lower than the angels
and potentially higher than the beasts. This poignant description
captured the lost dynamic in human life and experience. A fundamental contrast between nature and freedom constitutes the
human person's status.

Another philosopher unfairly blamed for this dualism was the
German thinker, Immanuel Kant. Kant attempted to restore the
dynamic moral person affirmed by Pascal and a few poets. He

posited a duality between the empirical self and the noumenal self. The empirical self denoted the human being's involvement in natural necessity; the noumenal self denoted that aspect of the human person free from such necessity and endowed with moral freedom. In this respect he developed a contrast similar to Pascal's. Unfortunately, Kant failed in his task because the model of nature current in his time was the mechanistic one derived from Newton and he worked within such a framework. So an even deeper alienation developed between mechanistic nature without feeling, value, emotion and the moral freedom of the human being. As a result, moral freedom devoid of aesthetic elements became austere and formal; it was thus a rather poor reflection of the mechanism it was trying to avoid.

The Pascalian contrast was recaptured to some extent by G. W. F. Hegel in his *Early Theological Writings* and also in his *Phenomenology of the Spirit*. Hegel was, however, hampered by the given, intractable paradigms of nature available to him, and the dynamic perspective he posited in his dialectical philosophy suffered as a result.

One of Hegel's less gifted disciples philosophically, but his outstanding critic theologically and spiritually, borrowed the dialectical contrast between finitude and infinitude from him and produced a profound psychological study of the human person called *The Sickness Unto Death*. Søren Kierkegaard's analysis of the dynamics of the human self in that work anticipates much that has been taught in this century by dynamic and depth psychology. It is a remarkable achievement in that the human person is no longer seen as some kind of static soul-substance alongside a static body-substance. Rather the human person is a vibrant experiential reality relating itself to itself in the contrast between its finitude as body and its infinitude as spirit. The two aspects of the contrast are equally affirmed. So in this creative tension we begin to understand more fully what the human spirit is all about.

An unfortunate neglect can be detected in Kierkegaard's thought which is due to his own personal struggle. He was unable to affirm the spiritual dynamic he articulated in his relationship with other human beings. As a result, the exclusive focus is on an isolated, alienated, despairing human being, relating itself to itself, and to the God revealed in Jesus Christ. This neglect of the social dimension has been a deficiency found in much later existentialist reflection with the exceptions of Martin Buber and Gabriel Marcel.

In Kierkegaard, one of the fundamental contrasts within life and experience resulting in spirit was found; the contrast between finitude and infinitude. The human being in such a perspective, however, was the alienated soul of Descartes relating to itself in isolation from nature and other human beings.

What is needed is precisely a philosophical and theological explanation which does full justice to the human being as a dynamic self of relationships seeking a personal center or identity, and thus becoming a vibrant spiritual being. We should also find a way in which such a dynamic human being can be related to nature, no longer itself conceived as a realm of fixed necessity, a machine, but rather understood as a rhythmic, pulsating organism made up of a vast number of moments of experience, pulses or energy-units.

It would also be advantageous to find a way in which the human being, no longer alienated from nature, can relate itself to other human beings in the kind of social experiments which avoid as much as possible the separation of person from person. We need to foster the development in other words of interpersonal, mutually interdependent social structures. And finally we should develop an approach in which the relating to God can be co-ordinated with views of nature and human beings, so that communion rather than isolation, adventure rather than passive conformity, risk rather than apathy, can be the hallmarks of the spiritual quest.

The Dynamic Human Person As Model

Even though it is an expression of wisdom discovered by human beings after much struggle that the human perspective is not and cannot be absolutely definitive for what is the case, the human perspective, nevertheless, is where we must begin. We cannot avoid that since our initial contacts with reality are focused by the human perceptual apparatus. This is the truth in the philosophical meditations of Descartes about the certainty to be found in looking within, and affirming the I think, therefore I am (*cogito, ergo sum*).

Arrogance has often prevailed making human perceptions of reality totally definitive. Presumably, it did not enter the mind of Descartes that other sentient beings might have different perspectives, and thus within their ability to do such things, draw different conclusions. Dogs and bats have a broader range of perceptual ability as far as audition is concerned in that they can hear sounds human beings cannot. But if human arrogance were to have its way no sounds could be heard which escape the human perceptual ken. The verse which Whitehead quotes in his book *Modes of Thought*[1] about a nineteenth century Master of Trinity College, Cambridge, Illustrates this point:

> *I am the Master of this College*
> *And what I know not,*
> *Is not knowledge*

Ralph Barton Perry, an American philosopher, identified this as the egocentric predicament. This predicament is most obvious when the alienated soul or substance, needing nothing but itself and perhaps God to exist, achieves centrality in philosophical, theological and even spiritual disciplines. The solution to such a predicament is not easy to find. This is true because the human perspective which is the problem also constitutes the only starting point available for the human being.

What, then, can be done? We need first to affirm the obvious, that is, that human beings perceive what they perceive, experience what they experience. As a result of this affirmation, we should reflect on the data derived from such perceptions and experiences and attempt to construct a framework which accounts for the peculiar characteristics of human experience. At the same time such a framework would see human experience as a rather sophisticated expression or focus located within a much broader experiential matrix. This kind of exercise in imaginative reflection should result in the liberation of human beings from their egocentric predicament, at least philosophically and scientifically. Perhaps simultaneously, it would enable human beings not only to affirm their perceptions and experiences as starting points, but also as eventual points of departure in their reflective and spiritual quest.

An important truth coming out of such a reflective and spiritual quest is that consciousness (human and nonhuman) presupposes a vast experiential matrix from which it arises, and that human consciousness is itself only the very tip of that experiential iceberg. Human conscious experience is, therefore, not the initial stage, but rather a highly complicated and sophisticated stage of experience emerging from the vast experiential abyss shared in various ways by all sentient and nonsentient beings. Consequently, human conscious experience presupposes that vast area of unconscious experience.

The question is: How do we describe such a vast area of unconscious experience so that all that is distinctive in conscious human experience is both preserved and not distorted? We must place ourselves in a position so that we can see the highly delicate relativity that accompanies the emergence of human consciousness. Theologically, one could say that such an effort is the attempt to affirm the creatureliness of the human being as over against human pretensions aspiring to the status of angels.

A dynamic human nature is constituted by fundamental contrasts or tensions between finitude and infinitude, physical and mental, what has been or what is in contrast to what may be (facticity in tension with possibility). Such a dynamic human nature is not alienated from other beings of nature, but rather is a peculiarly structured focus or expression emerging from a vast experiential matrix. Such contrasts or tensions recognized on the human level can also be assumed to be implicit in some sense in a variety of ways in the experiential iceberg below the surface of human conscious perception.

This means that we can use the dynamic, human person as a model in our attempt to understand the vagaries of nature. This also means that we can do this without presupposing unbridgeable gulfs between the inorganic, the organic and human consciousness. The possibilities for kinship and communion with nature are thus affirmed, and because of the possibilities for kinship and communion the egocentric predicament is avoided.

Nature As Organized Feeling

Using the dynamic human person as a model, and being aware of the need to heal the dissociation of sensibility which alienates thinking and feeling from one another, it is necessary to engage in some imaginative reflection in order to describe that vast experiential matrix from which human consciousness is a sophisticated and delicate emergent. One of the important characteristics of total human experience is feeling.

We are often confronted with the suggestion that we should trust our own feelings. Feelings can be expressed in many ways.

The experience of being unable to verbalize certain feelings does not necessarily reflect a lack of linguistic skill. It may indicate vast areas of human feeling which are outside the clarity and distinctness of verbal formation. Such feelings are no less real, but when compared to the clarity and distinctness of words expressing the human reflective process, they are dim and vague. These same feelings, however, influence, more than we often realize, the restricted area of clarity which we call conscious experience. They determine mood, attitude, whether one is in a state of exhilaration, or one feels as though a heavy weight accompanies every conscious moment.

This vast area of feeling is channeled to us unconsciously through our various bodily functions. It is finally expressed as the dim and vague background of our conscious moments. An example of this can be drawn from the experience of gradually coming into consciousness when the anesthesia wears off after an operation. The vast feeling activity of the human body has been going on up to that point, but there has been no awareness at all. Then, there are a few flickerings of consciousness, yet still characterized by a certain dimness and vagueness. Finally, one recovers the clarity and distinctness of human consciousness. The human person is made up of such unconscious feelings, organized and finally focused or expressed in the moments of consciousness.

It should be obvious how much distortion can occur when we assume that only the conscious moments, and the clear and distinct ideas resulting from them, are the total human person. The distortion is most evident when this consciousness is then dissociated from that vast area of unconscious feeling presupposed as the very possibility of human conscious states. Such a dissociation results in what Basil Willey describes in *The Seventeenth Century Background*[2]: "Instead of being able, like Donne or Browne, to think and feel simultaneously, either in verse or in prose, you were now expected to think prosaically and feel poetically."

What we have been describing is the human being as a psychosomatic whole. The soul and the body are not alienated substances, but rather constitute one living, breathing, feeling and thinking organism, an incarnate reality. The experiential matrix from which the conscious moments arise is precisely the human body and its many relationships with the nature of which it is a distinct part.

From the reflective standpoint of the clarity and distinctness of the conscious moments, the human body has the character of a unified social structure. We should realize, however, that the bodily organism, as a unified social structure, is made up of many organs. These organs are themselves constituted by large numbers of structured cells each with its own nucleus; the cells are made up of molecules; and the molecules are socially organized wholes containing many atoms. Furthermore, the atoms can be broken down into protons, electrons, etc.; and the protons and electrons are themselves only intellectual approximations to the energy-units, or moments of experience, which perish as soon as they come to be. From this kind of analysis of the human organism as a unified social structure of organs, cells, molecules, atoms, et. al., it is possible for us to understand how below the level of human consciousness the body has an interdependent relationship with nature as this dynamic experiential or feeling matrix.

What is being posited here in this exercise of imaginative reflection is simply that conscious human experience is itself an expression of this vast matrix. Moreover, it is a distinct expression which achieves a self-direction, a self-consciousness, and this enables it to engage in reflection which can explain the framework from which it has arisen. Consequently, this makes the human conscious moments appear to be a little lower than the angels and certainly different from the beasts whose organized conscious moments do not permit them the degree of sophistication necessary for such reflection and inquiry.

We must now concentrate on some of the fundamental contrasts already discussed which characterize the human being. The tension between the physical and the mental, the unconscious and the conscious, the finite and infinite, are a selection from the many tensions or contrasts which serve to express the dynamics of human life and experience. We should use these tensions as ways of opening up the possibility of developing an imaginative sketch of the vast experiential matrix. It should also serve to elucidate the claim that nature is organized feeling.

From the perspective of conscious human experience, we are able to ascertain that the reflective or mental aspects of experience are clear, distinct and most prominent. In contrast the physical aspects assume a certain dimness and vagueness in comparison to mental or conceptual activity. Such dim and vague bodily activity asserts itself in conscious moments with poignancy, when pain due to an upset of organic equilibrium is felt. Otherwise, the body is only a dim and vague presence. Even in human perception, as contrasted to a more sophisticated human reflection, what is perceived are sense data, but these sense data have the character of universals such as color (e.g. redness), shape (e.g. squareness), texture (e.g. hardness), etc. In the perception of universals we are at a level of complicated conceptual ordering, and we perceive objects which are actually highly organized structures appearing to us as sense data.

Jan Christiaan Smuts in *Holism and Evolution* describes the objects of human conscious experience as energy stereotyped into structure. Such structures or stereotypes can be seen in the mountains, the rocks, the tables, and all other realities we perceive as objects of sense experience. These structures or stereotypes, furthermore, are clearly and distinctly conceptual or mental and dimly and vaguely physical. So if we are to understand the vast experiential matrix which is presupposed as the framework for such human conscious experience and its objects, we cannot use the objects of sense experience, the structures or stereotypes, as patterns for that which is below the level of such highly conceptual, conscious human experience.

Smuts says that such objects are energy stereotyped into structure. What, then, constitutes the energy which is stereotyped? We have described atoms as being made up of protons, electrons, etc. We have also seen that protons and electrons are imaginative intellectual constructions which attempt to capture what an energy-unit, a moment of experience, an actual occasion, can be understood to be. They are realities which perish as soon as they come into being. This is why it is impossible to deal with such units of energy as though they were perceptual objects.

Whitehead understands such moments of experience, actual occasions, energy-units, to be the true realities out of which all else is derived. In this respect, he is very near to Smuts and his energy stereotyped into structure. Whitehead, however, sees these energy-units as units of feeling, and this feeling has both a physical and a mental pole. The contrast between the physical and the mental which is so important in understanding the dynamics of human personhood is projected as present within the feeling-units, the moments of experience, the actual occasions.

Whitehead makes a sketch in which these feeling-units may be organized as electrons, protons, atoms, molecules, etc. In the initial organization or structuring of these actual occasions, or these moments of experience, the feeling-units take on the characteristics of being primarily conformal to past reality. In such conformity the physical is most prominent and the conceptual or mental is dim and vague. Here the social organization of such feeling-units is such that conformity prevails primarily. As a result the current units of feeling arising in the creative process find their direction or aim from the past units and conform to them.

At this stage of feeling-units being stereotyped into structure, we are dealing with the inorganic, that which is without life. The feeling-units themselves are dynamic moments of experience, but they are organized in such a way that social stability prevails through conformity to the structures. Crystals, for example, have the capacity to last longer than sensitive organisms. This is because conformal feeling is basic and the physical is paramount, while the conceptual is dim and vague. In crystals the finite is fundamental and the infinite is seen only vaguely within the overpowering weight of finitude; facticity is primary and possibility is all but lost. Conformal feeling, the primacy of the physical and the weakness of the mental, thus is superior in the realm of the inorganic.

When the conceptual or mental element ceases to be a dim aspect of the physical and begins to be seen as something in contrast to the physical, even if it is a very primitive contrast, we see the emergence of structures of feeling-units which are organic or living. The difference between the inorganic and the organic is a difference of social structure. In the former case, the social structure has the kind of character that places all feeling-units in a primarily conformal posture and thus promotes the social stability needed for the inorganic or lifeless objects. In the latter case, the social structure permits the beginning of a contrast or tension between what has been and what may be, facticity finds itself in tension with possibility, the finite is contrasted with the infinite.

In living structures social stability does prevail, but an uncertainty, a risk, an adventure towards the realization of the possible rather than a reproduction of the actual, asserts itself. Life is in Whitehead's thought a bid for freedom. Consequently, the physical, conformal and factual is contrasted with the mental, creative and the possible. The mental, creative and the possible, however, are dim and vague aspects of inorganic reality, only achieving more clarity and distinctness when the organic structures arise.

If we are able now to continue our exercise in imaginative reflection, we can perhaps understand how the living cells, made up of molecules, which are constituted by atoms, etc., can become more and more complex and sophisticated. As more complexity arises in organic development, it is accompanied by more risk, more adventure, more possibility. So, as a result, the conceptual or mental becomes more prominent, and the physical or conformal becomes in contrast dim and vague.

When consciousness arises in this process, the conceptual, the clear and the distinct, overshadows the physical; but the physical is not lost. The physical is there in a brooding, unconscious presence furnishing much that is now presupposed by consciousness. And thus with the development of human self-consciousness, the possibilities for reflection, for risk, for spiritual adventure, are magnified even more.

The human being who lives at a level of self-consciousness and who feels the intensity of the contrast between the physical and the mental, the finite and the infinite, the factual and the possible, is in comparison to a stone a socially deficient creature. Realities that are inert or inorganic are the most socially perfect in their structures, and these structures usually last indefinitely. When sensitivity, possibility, conceptuality, risk and adventure are contrasted with such social stability as a stone possesses, it becomes more obvious that the price paid for life, and for conscious selfhood, is the sacrifice of rigid social stability which results in social deficiency. When a person launches out into the unknown, that person sacrifices a stable security for an uncertain future. But life in its very essence is this sort of spiritual quest. It refuses to be embalmed alive! Life is indeed a bid for freedom; the human spiritual quest is a sophisticated qualification of such an elemental bid for freedom found in all living reality.

As a result, the human infant is one of the most vulnerable of creatures. Human infants are at birth more socially deficient than many other creatures. Most infant animals have built within their organic structure the kind of equipment needed for survival. Although alive, they have inherited physical, conformal structures that give them more social security at birth. They are less in need of care and nurture and more sufficient within their natural environment. Their bid for freedom is less intense. Thus the social structuring of many animal bodies is more stable and effective than what is found in the human infant.

Human infants are most vulnerable. They are unable to survive as human beings without a context of care and concern lasting over a period of several years. So from the beginning of human life, the spiritual quest is there; the human infant is a creative and spiritual possibility with all the risk and adventure implicit in such a socially, deficient creature.

Culture As Spiritual Nurture

People do not ordinarily think of inorganic objects such as stones as having a social structure, but the structuring or stereo-typing from the human perceptual level of the vibrant feeling-units results in a perceptual object, the stone. Such objects are the best approximation to social stability that we know.

We have seen that the human infant as a structured organism is socially deficient. The social deficiency, however, represents possibility, freedom, adventure and risk. It is also one of the necessary elements in the cultivation of a dynamic human person; organismic facticity or social stability in contrast to and in tension with human possibility or social deficiency.

This so-called social deficiency of the human infant is related to the need for a spiritual quest. The word, spirit, is intimately related to the pulsations and rhythms of life; it is itself derived from the Latin word, *spirare*, meaning to breathe or to blow. Spirit represents unpredictability or possibility when contrasted to socially rigid structures such as stones. Stones last for a long period of time, but their spiritual significance is minimal. In contrast to less stable structures, it is even trivial.

The presence of spiritual possibility occasions more intense experience. Spiritual activity dissociated from social structure or with little social structuring is soon burned up by its own intensity. Consequently, social structures, trivial in themselves, are needed as well as spiritual possibility. Spirited freedom is expressed through social structures, and thus the spiritual intensity is mediated in such a way that it does not become self-destructive.

We have seen that a spiritual quest is necessary for the human being from infancy onward. Because of the vulnerability of the human infant, artificial structures of a cultural nature must be developed for its care and nurture. Such artificial structures are the various social expressions that go to make up human culture. In this respect, human cultural exertion is itself a kind of spiritual activity. Its purpose should be the provision of the social structures needed for the nurture and actualization of spiritual possibility. The human infant thus has both a biological matrix from which it has arisen and a cultural matrix which is responsible for its care and its eventual emergence into a dynamic human person, living in the tension between facticity and possibility, finitude and infinitude, what is or has been and what can or may be.

To use a Biblical metaphor, the fleshpots of Egypt are often preferred to the uncharted wilderness of Sinai. As a result the models for the artificial social structures developed in cultural exertion often represent the kind of social stability found in the inorganic structures where stability is most secure. Even if organic models are used, they tend to represent social stability as paramount and spiritual possibility as minimal.

In the first instance, social stability based on the inorganic, we find that many mechanistic models for community in which each individual is seen as a distinct part or expression of the social structure itself. The smooth functioning of the social machine is the primary concern. As a result, such social structure becomes philistine or spiritless. The bid for freedom is neglected; and human life is transformed into a hopeless image of the inorganic. All this is done for the sake of social stability. Here the dead paradoxically live on; they also bury their own dead.

In the second instance, a certain minimal affirmation of life is affirmed since the model is organic rather than inorganic. Human spiritual possibility, however, is expressed in such a way that the social unit itself becomes the only true individual. All who are in it are only its particular manifestations. This model is not unlike the mechanistic one since it is a primitive form of organism which is being used here as a model (ants and bees). Social determination takes precedence over individual, spiritual possibility.

Models based on organism (the living) are preferable to those based on mechanism (the dead). Since the human infant is socially deficient from an organismic perspective, this may be an indication that artificial, cultural structures should not reflect either mechanical or organic models for community. On the human level we have a new kind of emergence which transcends to some extent both mechanism and organism. Novel structures are therefore needed! Here we see the human historical drama arising and the historical dimension transcends both mechanism and organism.

Culture, as spiritual nurture, should provide communities in which human personhood is delicately shaped. In such communities the nurturing structures representing social stability should be in a healthy tension with human freedom and the spiritual quest. Such a healthy tension should eventuate in communities in which an interpersonal or intersubjective dynamic is fostered. In these communities a mutual interdependence would be affirmed without occasioning pathological dependence. The artificial social structures of human culture, in other words, should be a support of the human spiritual quest, and not a hindrance to it.

Spirituality, Sin and Faith

The tensions resulting in vibrant human life and experience are often lost through a human arrogance which issues from the sins of pride and sensuality. Pride and sensuality have been explained well in the past by St. Paul, St. Augustine, and in our time, by Reinhold Niebuhr.

A simple explication is not easy, but pride is fundamentally a loss of finite perspective and a journey into fantasies of infinitude. The prideful person is unwilling or unable to affirm human creatureliness. As a result, the human bid for freedom is isolated from its emergence in finite nature, and the person plays out the fantasy of being an angel. Angelism is another word for the sin of pride.

Without its grounding in finite nature the human bid for freedom becomes fundamentally deficient. It is an expression of nothingness. As a result, the prideful person is constrained to fill up this emptiness. This occurs in a variety of ways but it usually takes the form of absolutizing some of the finite structures responsible for past care and nurture. These structures are then dissociated from the dynamics of life and history. Any finite, fabricated structure of culture can be selected, and the results of such choices are seen in the pretensions coming from a scientism, an aestheticism, a statism, a moralism, or an ecclesiasticism. The structure (or structures) selected, moreover, becomes a haven of rest from the responsibilities implicit in dynamic personhood. The angel/human being can rest secure in the fabricated zion of a human prideful state.

The sin of sensuality is directly related to pride. The emptiness of the prideful person is never assuaged, since it is a nothing or an infinity. Disillusionment with the fanciful secure structures that have been absolutized can drive the prideful self into a binge of finitude. In such a binge the person tries to fill up the nothingness of its prideful posture. The person attempts to pull all finite reality into himself or herself in a frantic effort to find fullness. Sensuality is basically this use of finitude as material for filling one's own emptiness, whether it expresses itself particularly in sexual excesses, drunkenness, drug addiction, gluttony, avarice and the like.

Pride and sensuality are two sides of the same coin. These fundamental sins express an alienation from other human beings, from nature and from God. They denote a state in which the human person, because of alienation and isolation, experiences no acceptance from others. Nature from which personhood has emerged is found to be foreign and ultimately destructive (death). God is often seen as a vengeful judge and as a capricious deity in need of all forms of oppressive satisfaction. St. Paul sums it up: As in Adam all die, a solidarity of alienation according to the flesh. In other words, reality is fundamentally alien and rejecting. Human life is a struggle to protect itself from such rejection and to find anywhere, even in fantasies if need be, the acceptance that is not discerned in reality itself.

The fanciful absolutized structures which attempt to enclose the infinite and secure it for those who are apparently in need are what the Marxists have called the opiates of the people. Both religious and political structures have been such opiates in the past and are deserving of criticism for their pretensions and their idolatries. The enclosure of the infinite takes on the social character of a stone. This enclosed infinite is where a person may find an ersatz peace and rest, or a living death. The bid for freedom is lost since no reality is permitted outside the finite enclosure of the infinite.

To illustrate this, two examples are in order. An *esprit de corps*, a social self, becomes the definitive expression for well defined groups. This social self in many instances becomes the only true person or individual, and the members of the group are expressions or aspects of the group's social self, a collegial spirit in which all of the colleagues are mere aspects. When such a group is defined to protect its members from all that is without, it simultaneously affirms itself as a kind of exclusive enclosure of the infinite. If this particular group has a religious structure, and if there is a charismatic leader for the group, then, this charismatic leader may become for the other members a literal embodiment, a kind of quasi-incarnation, of the group's social self, or in religious language, a god or a holy spirit. The members are totally under the spell of the leader.

On the other hand, if the structure takes on a more secular, political character, a totalitarian state may arise claiming to be the full enclosure of the infinite, the absolutized finite. Here the most obvious examples are the Nazi aberrations of the recent past and the Marxist claims of Stalin and Soviet totalitarianism.

Whether these structures are religious or political, they are indeed opiates of the people. One of the greatest opiates offered today is seen in the fanciful political pretensions of the Soviet state and its satellites. The visit of Pope John Paul II to Communist Poland, and the courageous stand of Hans Küng against the pretensions of his own church, are dramatic judgments on political and ecclesiastical attempts to enclose the infinite.

We find ourselves faced with these fundamental tensions in human life and experience. We also find that life within these tensions is truly the dynamic needed for responsible personhood which can result in the human spiritual quest. Any so-called spirituality which is an expression derived from such attempts to enclose the infinite is not a spiritual quest but actually the working out of a death wish. To live in such an enclosure is to live as though one were dead. It transforms human personhood into a mere facet of such an enclosure. Such a social structure is as secure as a stone, but it is devoid of life as the bid for freedom. The spirit cannot be so enclosed. It refuses to be entombed.

A simple statement about the meaning of the Gospel of Jesus Christ can be stated as follows: Ultimately, the One who created us is the One who also redeems us, the One who is the source of both being and worth. God is the creator and preserver of all humankind. Even though we face rejection all around us, we can be assured that God loves and accepts us; and that Divine love and acceptance is a judgment on our lack of faith and our pride and sensuality. When human beings affirm that Divine love and acceptance, they are able to live within the spirited tensions we have described. They have no need for enclosures of the infinite.

Faith is among other things an affirmation of the dynamic human person hovering between finitude and infinitude, physical and mental, what has been and what can or may be. The adventure, the risk, the bid for freedom, are all expressions of that faith in the transcendent love and acceptance of God. Such divine love and acceptance stands in judgment on all attempts to enclose the infinite and thus deny the dynamic spiritual quest of human beings. St. Paul sums it up: So in Christ shall all be made alive, a solidarity according to the Spirit.

Spirituality, God and Christ

We are in Christ, according to the Spirit, when we respond to the Divine Presence definitively revealed for us Christians in the events centering in the life of Jesus of Nazareth. Here Christians find the focal point in history for the mediation of the transcendent God in and through these events. These events themselves have occurred in a dynamic historical context.

The God revealed in Jesus Christ has also been disclosed in the events recorded in Hebrew Scriptures. The Exodus from Egypt under the leadership of Moses is a paradigmatic expression of the Divine Presence for the Hebrew and Jewish people. Furthermore, the prophets of Israel and Judah were specific reminders to that people of the God who could not be enclosed, of the God whose thoughts were not their thoughts. The prophets witnessed to the One God transcending the many finite structures of human fabrication, and in their witness the sinful pretensions of human persons were judged.

The God revealed through Moses, the prophets and Jesus of Nazareth, has also been at work from the beginning (*arche*) in nature and in human history. The dynamics of nature are media for the Divine Presence, and the fabrications of human culture may be such media also. The human person in responding to that Divine Presence in nature and in history finds that Presence to be definitive for the human spiritual quest.

St. Justin Martyr in the second century affirmed that the presence of God could be found in the Greek philosophers, particularly Plato. Early in the Christian experience some believers discovered the universality of that Divine Presence focused definitively and particularly in Jesus Christ. One of those believers was the author of St. John's Gospel.

In the Prologue to the Fourth Gospel we find the key to this universal Divine Presence and its mediation particularly in the historical event of Jesus. John borrowed the philosophical category of Logos, first used by the Greek philosopher Heraclitus, and later made prominent in the writings of the Hellenistic Jew, Philo of Alexandria. The Logos was the Word of the silent, mysterious One. The Logos broke the silence of eternity. It was the Word of creation, the Divine Presence expressed in and through the totality of God's creative work. The Word was responded to in various ways by human beings in history, and in particular ways by the Hebrew and Jewish people in their specific festivals celebrating the Covenant with the One so revealed and so mediated. For Christians in the fulness of time, that Divine Universal Word, that presence of God, was definitively expressed, made flesh in Jesus of Nazareth. In Jesus, God was with us in a unique way (Emmanuel).

The response to that unique focus of God in Jesus of Nazareth resulted in an overwhelming expression of the Spirit. The festival of Pentecost is a celebration of those events when the Divine Presence of God mediated in and through Jesus Christ opened up the fulness of the Spirit to us and for us. That same Spirit was from the beginning (*arche*) and all the spiritual responses to the Divine Word expressed in nature and history wherever they have occurred, are aspects of that same Spirit responding to the particular way the Divine Word was being incarnated and focused.

The Incarnation of the Word of God begins with God's act of creation and continues to be expressed in all the facets of that creative act found in a dynamic nature and in the ongoing historical drama. In terms of our understanding, the expression of the Incarnate Word and its spiritual possibilities for response are minimal in the area of the inorganic. More spiritual possibility emerges as organic structures develop in nature. Spirituality becomes more intense in the sensitivity expressed in the consciousness of animals, and it acquires a particular intensity in human self-consciousness and its response to the working of Word and Spirit in the totality of the creation. An incarnate spirituality is most intense for human beings in the revelatory disclosures which constitute the starting point for the great religious traditions that have their emergence in the human historical drama.

Within such an explanation as this, we are able with St. John, St. Justin Martyr and countless others to affirm the uniqueness of the Divine Presence incarnated in Jesus of Nazareth, that presence which made him the Christ. At the same time, we are able to affirm the Universal Word and Spirit with its manifold expressions in nature (matter, life, consciousness, human self-consciousness, etc.), and also in human history (the variety of philosophical, scientific, aesthetic, political, moral and religious expressions).

In Christian history, however, attempts to enclose the infinite, to claim the Universal Word and Spirit as our own peculiar possession, are many. Idolatrous claims which are contrary to the teachings of Jesus attempt to enclose the infinite (the Divine Presence) in Jesus himself. The Universal Word is understood to be exhausted in the events of Jesus, and spiritual responses outside the Christian context are deemed to be demonic, evil and splendid vices.

The Holy Spirit, universal in its character, is equated with the *esprit de corps*, the social self, of the Christian churches. Christian structures thus become the tomb of the Spirit. The enclosure of the infinite is often accomplished as we worship the One whose Spirit is supposed to transcend all human structures. Spiritual possibility has been at times absolutely defined and enclosed in the structures of the Christian religion. Such idolatries are common in all religious and political structural fabrications, but they should be resisted and a dynamic between structure and spirit, facticity and possibility, reinstated.

We have recounted two ways in which Christians particularly have attempted to enclose the infinite, to entomb the Spirit, or to absolutize the relative: first, in the reduction of the Universal Word and Spirit exclusively to the events centering in Jesus of Nazareth, and secondly, in the attempt to enclose the Holy Spirit in the structures of the churches. Christian *esprit de corps* becomes identical with the Holy Spirit.

A third way of enclosing the infinite can be found in those conceptions of God which upon close examination have a character similar to the stereotypes we have associated with inert objects such as stones. The God revealed in Holy Scripture is a living, dynamic reality who cares for the creation, who struggles and suffers on behalf of the creation, who in Jesus of Nazareth endured the cruelty and death of the Cross. The God of the Bible is a living God and a living God should not be described in impersonal or lifeless categories.

Traditional theology, however, has done just this. Static categories such as omnipotence, omniscience, immutability and impassibility, have been used to describe the Divine Reality. God is understood to be absolutely perfect and perfection is articulated in static terms. Actuality is a term acceptable for God, but possibility cannot be. Possibility in comparison to actuality reflects a deficiency and God by definition cannot be deficient.

Observations which have been made so far indicate that social deficiency is one of the important aspects of vibrant, living organisms in contrast to inorganic or inert stones. We have also suggested that human infants are socially deficient. Such social deficiency represents spiritual possibility, the lure of the uncharted, the lure of the not yet in comparison to the familiar and the actual. The dynamics of spirituality in the creation indicate the tension between actuality and possibility.

The conceptions of God which have dominated most theology are static ones, and even contrary to the God revealed in Holy Scripture. Our theological understanding needs to be more in line with the Bible and dynamic human experience. We need to insist upon a dynamic model for God rather than a God who is alienated and isolated from the dynamics of nature and historical human beings. We need to affirm what the static views rightly conserve in their articulations, but we must add other dimensions which have been neglected too often in past formulations.

Charles Hartshorne, an American philosopher, once said that God is that reality which surpasses all other realities, but God is also that reality which can from moment to moment surpass God. The unsurpassable God conserves the fidelity, the identity and the trustworthiness of the Divine Reality. In other words, God who is the source of all being is also the source of all good and of all worth for what is. Traditionally, God is both creator and redeemer, one God. The source of our being is not the enemy. As a result, we do not need a redeemer-god to rescue us from the creator-enemy god. The traditional perspectives have insisted rightly upon the eternity of identity, trustworthiness and fidelity in the Godhead.

That Divine Identity and Trustworthiness, however, should not be transformed into a static idol. God can surpass God. In other words, there is possibility for God as a dynamic, divine reality as there is in quite another sense possibility for human beings as dynamic persons. Our tradition has taught us that we are made in the image of God; that image should express both the actual and the possible.

When such models for God are accepted, this results in a vision of dynamic, Divine Reality transcendent in its eternity, but immanent in its accessibility to the dynamics both in nature and in history. God works in and through nature and history instead of being an isolated and alienated exception, a strange intruder, a gigantic hero-god rescuing us from the oppressively, evil world. God is with us (Emmanuel)! God, consequently, can find it possible to weep over Jerusalem, be a fellow sufferer, a companion who understands.

Such an understanding of God can rescue our models or concepts of God from becoming enclosures of the infinite. The Holy Spirit is an impossible anomaly theologically when concepts of a static God prevail. When actuality and possibility are articulated as creative tensions in the Divine Reality itself, the Holy Spirit which expresses that universal divine possibility is rescued in human understanding from its many fabricated tombs. The Holy Spirit is permitted to be its faithful but unpredictable self.

The fleshpots of Egypt, the social stability of a stone, the fabricated enclosures of the infinite, are all temptations for human beings in their spiritual quest. The lure of the Divine Grace opens up for us adventure, risk, the uncharted wilderness. Life, according to the Spirit, does not seek out tombs for a living death, but rather accepts the bid for freedom which is spiritual possibility, being in Christ.

Conclusion

It is hoped that this brief sketch of an incarnational spirituality will be useful to Christian pilgrims who are engaged in a spiritual bid for freedom. The suggestions offered are attempts to locate the human spiritual quest in the reality of nature and of history, and to present possibilities for spiritual discipline which do not presuppose the need for isolation and alienation from the world. Instead, the real need is for a healthy affirmation of that divine gift of the creation whose source is good and of worth to all. With this in mind, the following applications of such a sketch to a spiritual discipline may be in order.

First, creative tensions as described are not to be avoided but rather affirmed as genuine aspects of a dynamic personhood. A healthy anxiety is precisely what makes a person more sensitive and more human. Creative tension, healthy anxiety, should be nurtured within a posture of faith, and a spiritual discipline should be involved in the affirmation of such tensions. In contrast, a spiritual discipline which attempts to reduce reality, or to enclose the infinite, into a structure similar to an inert stone, results in a false tranquility, an ersatz peace. It is actually an entombment of the human spirit. Such an entombment of the spirit is also a denial of the mysterious workings of God's Holy Spirit. The peace which passes all understanding includes creative tensions, both the actual and the possible, and bears no resemblance to the many tempting opiates which are always available.

Secondly, much time is needed for contemplation and for intro-spection, and such periods of time should be provided in the person's schedule. But these times of personal quietness and re-treat should not be ways of isolating oneself from nature, and from other human beings. Instead, they should be used as oppor-tunities for developing a reconciling presence where communion and fellowship rather than lonely isolation is sought. Spiritual sensitivity, which is an expression of the dynamic creative tensions, should result in an open rather than a closed posture. In these moments of retreat the lures of the Divine Grace should be responded to, the lures toward creative and redemptive possi-bility, the affirmation of the bid for freedom.

Thirdly, a spiritual discipline should have its social or corporate dimension. Being in Christ is involvement with a solidarity of the spirit. Sensitivity to social questions should be fostered. One can-not affirm the bid for freedom if social structures which oppress and neglect other human beings are conveniently blotted out of one's consciousness. The spiritually disciplined person is a free person. And, moreover, a free person must pick up that option daily by standing against restrictive structures which attempt to stifle the human spirit, destroy the dynamics of human life, and transform fellow human beings into well behaved robots. Spiritual discipline needs no opiates, corporate or otherwise.

Fourthly, spiritual discipline obviously entails what traditionally has been a rule of life. But such a rule should itself be an out-growth from the dynamics of the human spiritual quest, and not a rigid stance which makes the word spiritual the opposite of a breath of fresh, exhilarating air. The rule of life should be constituted precisely by the affirmation of the creative tensions, the healthy anxiety, from within a posture of faith, from being in Christ.

Fifthly, liturgies for corporate worship should be sufficiently flexible and varied so that public worship does not resemble a congregation of the living dead visiting its corporate tomb. The 1979 *Book of Common Prayer* is a remarkable liturgical expression in that it provides flexibility, variety, traditional and novel structures for genuine worship.

And finally, a spiritual discipline should result in the affirmation of one's faith in that God incarnated in Jesus Christ; the One beyond the many and yet the One who is also with us; the One whose presence and grace is mediated sacramentally through the dynamic processes of nature and the events of human history; the One whose presence goes forth before us offering lures of possibility for increasing sensitivity and warmth, love and acceptance; the One whom we discover in our fellow creatures, human and nonhuman; the One who bids us feed the hungry, give drink to those who are thirsty, clothe the naked, heal the sick, visit those in prison; the One who is disclosed in the events of human history as our creator and redeemer; the One who conserves in eternity what can be conserved; and the One who is the faithful guarantor of meaning and worth for all creatures great and small.

Footnotes

[1] A. N. Whitehead, *Modes of Thought* (New York: The Free Press, 1968), p. 43.

[2] Basil Willey, *The Seventeenth Century Background* (Garden City, New York: Doubleday Anchor Books, 1953), p. 93.

An Afterword

William J. Wolf

Like a recurring theme in a symphony there emerges from this book the common conviction that Anglican spirituality is nourished by the *Book of Common Prayer*. "Anglican spirituality seems always to flow from the corporate experience of God in public worship and in community. The *Book of Common Prayer* is informative for Anglicans not only for definition of doctrine and polity but as well for the content and style of spirituality. That book is the matrix" (Siegenthaler).

In *The Spirit of Anglicanism* the Anglican way of being Christian was seen to involve "a liturgically and pastorally oriented dialogue between four partners, catholics, evangelicals and advocates of reason and of experience." It is not surprising that when the center of attention turns from Anglicanism as a Christian archetype to Anglican spirituality as such many of the defining elements of the former should reappear in various contexts and configurations now transformed in the crucible of prayer and liturgical celebration. The liturgical is at the heart of this spirituality whether explicitly in the common worship or implicitly in personal devotions. These latter reflect what the church does corporately and often recollect the events of the church's calendar or the Biblical story being read in the appointed lessons. Such classic Anglican manuals of devotion as Andrewes' *Preces Privatae*, Taylor's *Holy Living* and *Holy Dying*, Herbert's *The Temple* and Donne's prayers and sermons illustrate this linkage of personal devotion with the liturgical setting.

"Anglican spirituality arises out of the common prayer of a body of Christians who are united in their participation through physical presence and liturgical dialogue and sacramental action—in the cult in which the Church identifies itself as Church. It involves a corporate life whose times and seasons and offices and ordinances and readings and sermons are the means of corporate participation, in and through Christ, with God present to and for human beings in history in this world. Private devotion and prayer and

163

meditation on the part of individuals are supports for and means of putting oneself into and extensions of the ongoing, corporate, liturgical life of the Church" (Guthrie).

Seeking spiritual direction has become increasingly common in an ecumenical age, but a one-to-one relationship between a spiritual director and his or her "client" may foster a type of individualism that looks upon Bible, church and Prayer Book as simply "resources" for devotion. The "method" will miss the richness of Anglican spirituality which developed from and is always returning to the corporate, liturgical and sacramental fellowship of the church. To an Anglican seeking spiritual direction the advice might be: Enter fully into the life of the church with eyes and mind and heart open for in Anglican tradition it is the church itself in the totality of its life and liturgy which is the fundamental spiritual director.

This theme of "participation" is furthered by the study of contrition in Hooker, Donne and Herbert, a theme not appreciated enough today. Hooker pictured the aim of life as "participation in God through Christ by the Holy Spirit in the Church." This definition is deepened by his subsequent description of the Holy Communion: "The bread and cup are his bodie and blood because they are causes instrumental upon the receipt whereof the *participation* of his bodie and bloode insueth." In *The Temple*, Herbert wrote a pattern poem shaped like an altar and proceeded to show how contrition yields to praise as the altar of mere stone becomes the altar of the heart and then the altar of the Cross, enabling the soul to offer the sacrifice of praise and thanksgiving. Hooker, Donne and Herbert affirm that true praise, joy and thanksgiving proceed from that contrition which in turn is the gift of divine love.

The key to Thomas Traherne's appealing spirituality is an unusual combination of roles: mystic, poet and saint. Traherne's gift to us today is an "ecological mysticism" with a sense of *participation* in nonhuman forms of life based on the relatedness of all things. "You never Enjoy the world aright," says Traherne, "till the Sea it self floweth in your Veins, till you are Clothed with the Heavens, and Crowned with the Stars." Love is the bond of union between all creatures. "By Lov our souls are married and sodderd to the creatures." In his partially recovered notebook with liturgical meditations appropriate for the chief days of the church's year from Easter to All Saints we see how Traherne's own devotion has been shaped by the *Book of Common Prayer* and how he in turn sought to mold the meditation of others by its sacred disciplines of time and space. It might be said that he expressed the comprehensiveness of Anglicanism in an unusual form of mysticism—intuitive and yet intellectual, aesthetical and yet ethical, devotional and yet practical.

The English Evangelicals and Anglo-Catholics in spite of major differences in many areas shared in their spirituality a common quest for holiness, the first by the path of conversion and conformation to Christ and the second through a view of the church as communicating Christ in the sacraments by those standing in the apostolic succession. Maurice, who avoided party allegiances and even one based on his own principles, saw the need for reconciling the Anglican groups not as enemies, but as partners in dialogue. He developed a spirituality grounded in the universal law of sacrifice, a theme that in alliance with the Anglican emphasis upon the Incarnation would be repeated many times after him. Temple could write that the sacrifice of Christ was potentially the sacrifice of humanity and that our task, enabled by the Holy Spirit, is to take our place in that sacrifice. Temple's "reasonable" and practical spirituality can be illustrated by his statements that prayer is an expression of love, that where there is no love there can be no prayer, and that prayer, especially mutual intercession, is a great means of increasing the volume of love in the world.

Three at least of the partners to the Anglican dialogue described in *The Spirit of Anglicanism* have reappeared in this analysis of Anglican spirituality. The fourth, the advocate of experience, can be well illustrated by Evelyn Underhill who, beginning as a generalized mystic in her classic *Mysticism* (1911), developed into a committed Christian with special feeling for Christ's incarnation and sacrifice. All of this she brought to expression in *Worship* (1936). Underhill perceived God in three ways: (1) cosmic-ontological, (2) personal and (3) dynamic. These in turn corresponded in their complementarity to three aspects of the human self: (1) intellect, (2) feeling and (3) will. Again the three ways according to Underhill resembled the three persons of the Trinity and on the human side issued in: (1) adoration, (2) communion, and (3) cooperation. She saw worship as summed up in sacrifice, the action which expressed more fully than any other a person's deep if uncomprehended relation to God. Sacrifice, integral to primitive cultures, waited the full disclosure of its meaning in "the absolute oblation of the Cross."

". . . Christian spirituality consists of three parts or elements. First, there is that which Owen Chadwick calls 'interiority,' the source of the dynamic power in the Oxford Movement. This is that which the Evangelicals pointed to when speaking of conversion, that which Newman referred to when telling of the invisible world encroaching on the visible. Maurice spoke of 'Christ in every man' and the law of sacrifice, Temple of constant fellowship with God, and Underhill of cosmic-ontological awareness. Secondly, there is the expression of interiority in piety, formal worship, ritual and ceremonial, Word and Sacraments, and the corporate nurturing activity of Christians gathered as the church. This is that to which Underhill referred when speaking of communion. Finally, there is the expression of interiority in service, in sacrificial love directed not only to others in the church, but to others in the world at large, for the alleviation of suffering and through social action to change the structures of society for the sake of human freedom, fellowship and service, as Temple said" (Booty).

The liturgical orientation of Anglicanism and the corporate context of Anglican spirituality can be described in such a way that they come to define the Communion itself. "Discussion of ultimate reality in Anglicanism has not taken the form: How can my understanding conform to a statement which is taken to be a normative guide in such an inquiry? Rather, it has taken the form (arguably a more intellectually exciting and religiously believable form): What must reality be like if we pray and praise in this way?" (Stevick). The one liturgy, however, does not translate into simply one spirituality where the individual is concerned; the one liturgy really implies many spiritualities. This will be especially true of the new *American Prayer Book 1979* with its many options, choices and alternative forms. "The church can have a just role in shaping the church's prayers; it has no comparable responsibility or competence in directing the private prayer of each member. Yet by setting forth a rich, generous liturgy for corporate worship, all derivative private or group prayer will be given an inspiration and a standard" (Stevick).

Music too is an expression of Anglican spirituality. It helps to keep a congregation together and to raise people's spirits to a mystical level for converse with the timeless. In chanting, for example, the timelessness may be expressed in the mantra-like repetition of the music, combined with the rhythm of the words and the dying away in volume at the mediation and final ending of the line. Here too, the testimony is the same. "Anglican spirituality is rooted in the Church's liturgical life. Liturgical music serves two purposes: it is an offering of praise in the context of the liturgy and it enhances the liturgy" (Cassels-Brown).

Skinner analyzes the dualism explicit or implicit in nearly every current philosophical attempt to understand the human situation. He would agree with Basil Willey that instead of being able like Donne or Browne to think and feel simultaneously in verse or prose the modern person was now expected to think prosaically and to feel poetically. Using the type of holistic analysis pioneered by Whitehead, Skinner charts a course for reflection on Anglican spirituality to take in expressing its favorite doctrine of the incarnation. He senses danger whenever a group to protect itself from all that is without or beyond the group affirms itself as a "kind of exclusive enclosure of the infinite." "Our theological understanding needs to be more in line with the Bible and dynamic human experience. We need to insist upon a dynamic model of God rather than a God who is alienated and isolated from the dynamics of nature and historical human beings . . . God, consequently, can find it possible to weep over Jerusalem, be a fellow-sufferer, a companion who understands" (Skinner). Such an incarnational spirituality can interpret the centrality of the church and its liturgy, the incarnation, participation, thanksgiving, sacrifice and openness to the Holy Spirit in a renewed kind of spirituality.

Anglican spirituality, deriving its orientation from the liturgical use of the *Book of Common Prayer* and from recollection on that relationship and the Biblical story and Gospel underneath it all can be summed up in Underhill's trilogy: adoration, communion and cooperation. We make growth in spirituality when we wrestle simultaneously with these elements in our everyday experiences and when we recognize thankfully the same dynamic activities in our fellow pilgrims on the way and in that greater company who have gone before us. "Underhill's phrase, 'atmosphere of God,' covers all three and for Anglicans, without denying exceptions and without making exclusive, absolute claims as to the validity of what we know and cherish, that atmosphere is best found in the church and its worship. In the Eucharist there is given with great clarity and objectivity the revelation of God in Christ, there is

experienced communion with one another in Christ, and there is
released the power of the Holy Spirit to change the world. Christ
on the cross exhibits to us the sacrificial love of God and reveals
the law of our humanity. Christ in the sacrament enters into
communion with us, forgiving our sin and empowering us to new
life. Christ in the faithful communicant goes forth to love and
serve the world as a whole . . ." (Booty).

The General Thanksgiving from the *Book of Common Prayer*
sums up very well the reality of Anglican spirituality.

> *"give us such an awareness of your mercies,*
> *that with truly thankful hearts we may*
>   *show forth your praise,*
> *not only with our lips, but in our lives,*
> *by giving up ourselves to your service,*
> *and walking before you*
> *in holiness and righteousness all our days."*